GOLF DOCTOR

GOLF
DOCTOR

John Jacobs
with Dick Aultman

Foreword by Jack Nicklaus

The Lyons Press

First published in the United States as *Curing Faults for Weekend Golfers* in 1979 by Simon and Schuster

First Lyons Press edition—1999

Printed in the United States of America

10 9 8 7 6 5 4 3 2 1

Library of Congress Cataloging-in-Publication Data

Jacobs, John, 1925–
  [Quick cures for weekend golfers]
  Golf doctor / John Jacobs with Dick Aultman; foreword by
Jack Nicklaus.—1st Lyons Press ed.
    p. cm.
  Originally published: Quick cures for weekend golfers.
New York: Simon and Schuster, 1979.
  ISBN 1-55821-795-9
  1. Golf. I. Aultman, Dick. II. Title.
GV965.J338 1999
796.352'3—DC21   98–45080
                   CIP

CONTENTS AND LESSON GUIDE

FOREWORD

BECOMING A GOOD GOLFER requires a variety of talents, some innate, some acquired. In the area of innate talents, I was blessed with excellent coordination, a strong pair of legs and a love of competition, and there is no doubt those three factors have contributed very heavily to my record in the game.

I'm certain, however, that no such record would have been possible without certain acquired abilities. All of these are important, but in my mind one stands out well ahead of all the others. All the great champions have possessed it. It is a total understanding of golfing cause and effect: a precise knowledge of exactly what is required in terms of club/ball impact to make a golf ball travel in a particular manner.

Unfortunately, no one is born with that knowledge. It has to be acquired. One of the luckiest events of my life was finding a teacher, Jack Grout, who not only could impart that knowledge, but insisted upon doing so ahead of everything else. Jack simply would not let an ambitious young pupil move along with the physical "how" until he totally mentally comprehended the "why" of his actions. With Jack, you had to know your *objectives* before you attempted to swing the club. Otherwise, he reasoned, the only thing you could depend on getting from the game in the future would be fresh air and frustration.

It is that same unrelenting insistence on understanding and applying the fundamental objectives of the swing, plus his remarkable ability to explain them clearly, that makes John Jacobs such a great golf teacher. Most golfers either never learn the true objectives of the swing in terms of club/ball impact, or increasingly overlook them in their concern with the particularities of the action.

Using the flight of the ball as incontrovertible evidence of how the club strikes it, Jacobs forces them back to the basic laws of impact, which are the only starting point for genuine and permanent improvement. Because his logic is unarguable and his reasoning so understandable, his success rate with all levels of golfers from beginner to tournament player has been and continues to be outstanding.

Certainly the most sought-after teacher in Europe, and increasingly in demand in the United States, John's previous books have been enormously popular on both continents. I am sure that this extremely practical volume will be equally successful.

JACK NICKLAUS

INTRODUCTION: HOW YOU WILL BE TAUGHT

THROUGHOUT THE YEAR I teach many groups of golfers who have gathered from all over the world to improve their games. On the first morning of such a school, I sometimes perform a little demonstration on the lesson tee that always seems to capture the students' attention.

First I ask for a volunteer to step forth from the group. I ask for someone who has played the game for some time but who I have never before seen swing a club.

Then I step to the forward part of the tee and off to one side. Facing down the range with my back to that pupil, I ask him or her to hit some tee shots down the range in full view of the entire class.

I watch only the flight of the ball, not the player's swing, for one or two shots. Then, while I continue to look away from the pupil, I will ask one of my assistants to see that the student makes one or two simple adjustments.

Inevitably, the pupil's shots improve immediately. Someone who has sliced his drives all his life suddenly hits a shot that draws slightly from right to left. Others who have frequently lobbed tee shots high into the air a relatively short distance now drive the ball forward on a much more penetrative trajectory an additional 20 or 30 yards.

The reason for this demonstration, and my purpose in describing it here, is simply to show that the golf ball itself is your best instructor. It is the teacher *extraordinaire* for two reasons (apart from its obvious availability):

First, the ball is extremely truthful and candid, often brutally so. It never lies or misleads (as golfers so often, inadvertently, do to themselves). It tells you straightaway on every shot exactly what your clubhead was doing at impact.

This is extremely vital information. Above all else it forms the basis for any meaningful, lasting improvement in your game.

The messages that we get from the ball are visual. We see its direction of takeoff. We see its direction and degree of sideways curve. We see its upward-downward trajectory and the distance it travels.

One of the main objects of this book will be to help you translate these visual messages. I hope to explain how you can learn from what your golf ball does. I will also suggest how to apply this knowledge, not only to improve your shots generally but also to avoid those extended periods where they go from bad to worse.

It is an unfortunate fact of golf that one bad shot frequently causes us to make incorrect adjustments. These lead to other, even more disastrous bad shots. This compounding of the original error is, indeed, a curse that all too often plagues the relatively unenlightened weekend player.

The best golfers also make bad shots. However, because the ball's flight alerts them to the true problem, they can usually correct the error early on, before it becomes compounded.

In this book I will also try to take you beyond mere corrections. I will attempt to explain how you can better control what your golf ball does and, thereby, better cope with the many situations that all of us inevitably encounter on the course.

The second reason why the golf ball teaches so well is that it is free of preconceived notions about golfing technique. It does not know or care if you hold the club in the "weak" grip position used by Johnny Miller or in the "strong" position favoured by Billy Casper. It doesn't know or care if you align to the left like Mr. Trevino or to the right like Mr. Locke. It isn't concerned if you play it forward in your stance as did Mr. Hogan or back as did Mr. Cotton. It doesn't even care if you keep your left arm as straight as Arnold Palmer's or retain your wrist cock as late as does Gary Player.

No, all that matters to the ball is what your clubhead does to it. Your shots, for good or bad, are determined by your impact conditions. Was your clubhead moving to the left or right or straight down your target line when it encountered the ball? Was the clubface facing to the left or right, or straight down that path? Was the clubhead moving down, up or parallel to the ground at impact? Was it travelling at a relatively fast or slow speed?

This is not to say that we do not determine our impact conditions by the way we hold the club, set up to the ball and actually swing. We certainly do. The point I'm stressing is that the ball can help enormously to show you what you should change in your own technique in order to improve your shots. It is a far more personal guide than some rigid gospel that is meant to fit all players into the same mould. I would suggest that you never accept a piece of instruction, no matter how enticing, without first asking just how this advice will improve your clubhead's impact with the ball.

To meet your individual needs, my instruction in this book may at times seem to differ from what you have come to accept as orthodox golfing technique. I hope that this will not concern you in the least.

In many instances my suggestions that seem and feel unorthodox to you will actually make your golfing technique *more* orthodox. The change to the orthodox will feel unorthodox to you only because that which had felt comfortable and orthodox actually was not. So often in golf the things we feel we are doing are quite different from what we are really doing.

Moreover, you should not be concerned if my suggestions to you really do, in fact, depart from the orthodox. It is somewhat unfortunate that throughout the history of the game golfers such as yourself have looked on the great players of the day as examples of how they should hold the club, address the ball and swing. Indeed, even the teaching profession itself has frequently used the words and examples of great players in determining the techniques that their own pupils should follow.

Using outstanding golfers as models for the way that everyone should play can be misleading for two reasons.

First, the great players have developed, through years of practice and play, certain physical capabilities and talents that the average club golfer not only lacks but quite probably will never develop.

Second, almost all of the great golfers I have known were players who, early on in their careers, flew most of their shots in a right-to-left pattern. Naturally these golfers developed techniques of grip, setup and swing that avoid hitting shots too far to the left.

Most club golfers, however (I would say at least 80 percent), are in the exact opposite situation. Their long shots usually curve from left to right. They need to develop techniques that will help them avoid hitting shots too far to the right.

Obviously a golfer whose trouble is slicing shots to the right might well aggravate that problem by applying the anti-hook techniques developed by the better players.

This is not to say that I reject the methods used by great players in my teaching. I merely want you to understand why I may, on occasion, suggest that you depart from certain of their techniques to some degree if your needs and skills differ from theirs.

Again, what really should concern you is merely improving your own personal set of impact conditions as reflected by the pattern of your shots.

Thus in this book I feel I shall be in partnership with the ball to help you improve, just as I am when teaching face-to-face.

The first section upcoming is extremely important. Like my opening remarks to a group of students, it explains how your impact conditions affect your shots. If you can absorb this basic information, you will find it much easier to apply the instruction of the succeeding lessons.

Each of these lessons will follow the same format that I use when teaching an individual after he has heard my opening remarks. This format breaks down into three parts—diagnosis, explanation and correction.

First, I watch the pupil hit a few shots. I stand so that I am facing directly down his target line. This view lets me see the path of his clubhead as it moves through the impact area. It also lets me see the ball's flight, including its initial direction of take-off and its direction and degree of sideways curve thereafter. This view of the shot, when combined with my observation of the clubhead's path, tells me where the clubface was facing at impact. It is at this point in the lesson, knowing what the club is doing to the ball and what the player is doing to the club, that I make my *diagnosis*.

Second, I give the pupil an *explanation* of what his club is doing at impact as well as what it should be doing if he is to improve. I may actually hit some demonstration shots. Initially I will reproduce the pupil's impact conditions and, naturally, my shots will resemble his. Then I will hit a shot or two on which I achieve proper impact conditions, to show the pupil how an improved set of conditions will similarly improve his shots.

Finally, I tell the pupil what *correction* of technique will improve his impact conditions. Usually I will also demonstrate the correction.

Diagnosis. Explanation. Correction.

Since I cannot be on hand to personally demonstrate for you the explanation and correction phases of the lessons in this book, I hope that you will pay close attention to the illustrations. They are designed to serve this purpose in my absence.

Also, since I cannot be on hand to observe your shots, you will need to diagnose yourself to some extent. To help you do this, I will start each lesson by describing a certain pattern of shots or a certain shotmaking situation. For instance, I may say "long shots start to the left of target on a low trajectory and then curve to the right, but short shots often fly—and remain—to the left with little or no subsequent curve to right."

If this diagnosis fits your particular situation, then the accompanying explanation and correction will apply to you.

To help you find the instruction that serves your particular needs, each lesson diagnosis is given in detail in the Contents and Lesson Guide at the front of this book.

The explanation portion of each lesson will, again, deal primarily with the influences of the club on ball. I will explain, for example, why it is possible to intentionally slice—but impossible to hook—a long shot around a tree from a tight lie. I will also tell you why it is very difficult—almost impossible—to slice a short shot around that same tree, even from a good lie.

I shall try to make your task of understanding and applying the correction portion of each lesson as easy as possible. I will often include a shortcut or practice tip that will further simplify your efforts. Finally, where applicable, I will also describe the pattern of shots that will result if you do, in fact, overcorrect.

Whereas the lessons in this book are designed to improve your shots, I believe that golf is more than mere shotmaking. It is also important, especially for the weekend golfer, to understand how to handle various on-course situations. Therefore I have also included in this book a section in which I describe such situations that so often lead to wasted strokes. I suggest ways to best avoid that happening.

Now we will proceed to the section that, as I stressed earlier, contains the meat of my thinking about impact and, thus, shot control. I do hope you will study this section carefully before proceeding farther into the book.

IMPACT FACTORS YOU SHOULD UNDERSTAND

I SOMETIMES RECEIVE phone calls from former pupils.

"John," the caller might say, "I've lost it. I'm back in trouble. I've tried everything—holding my head steady, changing my stance. I even bought a new set of clubs. Nothing helps."

Inevitably I respond, "Do not tell me what *you* are doing. Tell me what your *shots* are doing."

If my harried friend can accurately describe the pattern of his shots, I can usually help him straightaway. It doesn't take a miracle, just an understanding of what his golf club is doing at impact—this I can determine from his shot descriptions—plus some knowledge of his swing tendencies, which I can usually recall from having taught him at some time in the past.

To me these phone calls reflect a problem that faces most golfers. Most do not understand what their golf club is doing at impact with the ball to cause the pattern of shots they they hit. Because they do not know what their particular impact conditions are, they cannot know how they must be changed if their shots are to improve. Naturally, the player who does not know exactly how his impact conditions might be improved finds it extremely difficult to improve them.

True, such a player can try to improve his grip, address position and swing in all different ways that he has been told or shown or has read are ideal. Seldom, however, given such a wide choice, will he happen to attempt—and also correctly apply—the specific change or changes that would correct his particular impact faults. In fact, the changes that he makes will frequently accentuate these faults and even create new ones.

In this section I will try to provide the most basic information that you will need in order to realize, after looking at your shots, just what your particular impact conditions are. In the lessons and on-course situations that follow, I will expand on this information and also suggest the corrections that would most likely improve your particular impact situation.

Now I will start by explaining four factors, all occurring when the clubhead meets the ball, that affect your golf shots. I call these factors *clubhead path, angle of approach, clubface alignment* and *clubhead speed.*

As we shall see, these four impact factors combine to determine the shot's initial takeoff direction, its degree and direction of sideways curve thereafter, its upward-downward trajectory and, finally, its length.

CLUBHEAD PATH   If your clubhead is not moving straight toward your target when it strikes the ball, it must be moving toward the left or right of that goal.

If it is moving toward the target, it will be passing along the "target line," the imaginary line from ball to target. We refer to this clubhead path as being, simply, "on line" (*Illustration 1*).

If it is moving toward the right of the target at impact, it must be crossing the target line from the "inside"—your side of that line—to the "outside," or far side. This would be called an "in-to-out" path (*Illustration 1*).

If it is moving to the left of the target, it must be crossing the line from outside to inside on an "out-to-in" path (*Illustration 1*).

(If, Dear Reader, you happen to be among the minority that play golf left-handed, I'm afraid you will need to reverse the "lefts" and "rights" in this book. Thus, in this instance, an in-to-out path of movement, for you, would be toward the left of the target and an out-to-in path toward the right.)

The clubhead's path of movement at impact influences shots primarily by determining the direction in which the ball takes off (*Illustration 1*). If it starts out on target, regardless of where it curves thereafter, you may assume that your clubhead path was on line at impact. Shots that start out to the left, again disregarding where they curve afterward, indicate an out-to-in path. If your shots start to the right, you may assume that you are swinging in to out.

It is important that you understand not only these influences of the clubhead's path at impact, but also the clubhead's overall path before and after. Most importantly, you should realize that, *because in golf we stand to the side of the ball, the clubhead does not move on a straight line*. Instead, it must arc to the inside of the target line during the backswing. It must arc back to the target line during the downswing and, thereafter, arc back to the inside again during the follow-through.

Thus for the clubhead to move on line at impact, it must move *from* the inside and then back *to* the inside—in to in—before and after striking the ball. It can move on line with the target for only a very short span—a few inches at best—before returning to the inside.

This pattern of clubhead movement is similar to that of a swinging door, the type we frequently have seen in saloons in Western movies or in British pubs (*Illustration 2*). The door's outer edge arcs away from the doorframe as it opens, returns to the frame as it closes and then arcs away from the frame once again as it opens in the opposite direction.

Visual evidence of the swing's in-to-in nature is readily apparent in the divot marks on the tee of a par-3 hole after a day of play in a professional tournament. Since these good players take

Clubhead Path

1

Outside
(Other side of target line)

Target Line

On-Line Path
(Ball starts out on target.)

In-to-Out Path
(Ball starts out to the right.)

Out-to-In Path
(Ball starts out to the left.)

Inside
(Golfer's side of target line)

2   **Overall Path (Forward Swing)**

Ballistics of Ball Positioning

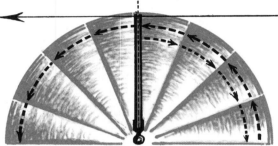

(Club moves from the inside, to the target line and then back to the inside—in-to-in overall—just as a swinging door does.)

3a

Ball Forward
(Club moving *to* inside; ball starts out to the left.)

3b

Ball Back
(Club moving *from* inside; ball starts out to the right.)

4

Club Moves In to In on All Full Shots

Longer Club (Driver)
(The in-to-in arc is more pronounced.)

Shorter Club (Wedge)
(The in-to-in arc is less pronounced.)

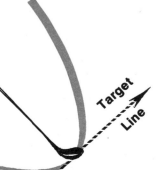

Target Line

Target Line

the divot just after impact, scars in the ground will arc from straight ahead to left of target, thus proving that the clubhead path through the hitting area is from inside, to along, to inside again.

Because the clubhead must travel on an arc rather than a straight line, the positioning of the ball is most important. Speaking strictly from a ballistic point of view, apart from any offsetting compensation by the player, if the ball is too far back in the stance—it's too far to the player's right and the player is too far to the left—the club will arrive at impact too early. It will still be moving in to out, *from* the inside and thus *toward* the right of target. The shot will start out in that direction (*Illustration 3b*).

Conversely, playing the ball too far forward, or left, in the stance—again speaking ballistically—makes the clubhead contact it too late. The club will have already begun its return *back to* the inside—toward the left of the target—and the shot will take off in that direction (*Illustration 3a*).

Thus, apart from any adjustment that the player might make in his or her swing, we have the general rule of impact ballistics that says, "Ball played back, shots start right; ball played forward, shots start left."

Finally, I wish to stress that the in-to-in path of clubhead movement applies on all full shots. While the clubhead does arc inside to a lesser extent on shots with the shorter-shafted clubs—because these clubs force us to stand closer to the ball— even on normal wedge shots there still should be some degree of in-to-in arc (*Illustration 4*). Even on these shots we are still standing to the side of the ball.

ANGLE OF APPROACH   Just as standing to the side of the ball dictates that the clubhead's path be an in-to-in arc, the fact that the ball is resting below our shoulders demands that the club also swing upward, downward and then upward again. Between the downswing and upswing phases, the clubhead reaches the bottom of its arc where, again for a brief span, it is moving more or less level (*Illustration 5*).

Thus it is obvious that if your clubhead is not moving level into the ball, it can be moving only on a downward or upward angle of approach.

I explained earlier how the ball's position in relation to the player affects the clubhead's *path of movement* at impact. So too does ball positioning affect the club's *angle of approach*.

Again speaking strictly about impact ballistics without regard for any swing adjustment by the player, when the ball is positioned relatively far back in the stance the clubhead reaches it relatively early, while it is still travelling rather downward (*Illustration 5*). The ball played forward, however, affords a later contact, by which time the clubhead will be moving less downward, if not upward (*Illustration 5*).

If contact occurs too early, when the clubhead is still moving steeply downward, much of its force is then applied to the ball in a downward direction, rather than forward. This misdirection of force immediately reduces the length of the shot (*Illustration 6*).

The angle of approach that is too steeply downward will also affect the trajectory of the shot. Under normal circumstances, shots played off grass fly lower than normal because the downward angle of approach, in effect, reduces the club's loft (*Illustration 6*). This downward angle may, however, produce the occasional, ineffective, higher-than-normal shot with wooden clubs when the ball is teed. The clubhead chops downward beneath the teed ball and contacts it high on the clubface (*Illustration 6*).

Given solid contact, the downward angle of approach is acceptable, if not preferable, on shots made with the more-lofted iron clubs. These clubs have enough loft, even when moving downward, to give the shot sufficient height. Also, they are used in situations where extreme length of shot is not the primary goal.

When impact occurs too late in the swing, when the clubhead has already started moving upward, solid contact becomes very difficult if the ball is sitting down in the grass. The club often catches the upper portion of the ball, which then dribbles along the ground (*Illustration 7*). Or the club contacts grass on the wrong side of the ball, behind it, having already reached the bottom of its arc at that point (*Illustration 7*).

The slightly upward angle of approach is, however, suitable on drives. Because the ball is teed, the upward sweeping clubhead can contact it solidly without first catching in the turf (*Illustration 7*).

Thus golfers who tend to sweep their shots with a shallow or upward angle of approach are usually at their best with the driver but poor with the medium and short irons where ball-then-turf contact is ideal. Conversely, golfers who swing on a very steep, downward angle of approach are usually poor drivers but fairly effective with the shorter irons.

At this point I would like to explain the direct and important relationship between the clubhead's path of movement and its angle of approach. First let us take the in-to-out path:

The swing that returns the clubhead to the target line from

Angle of Approach

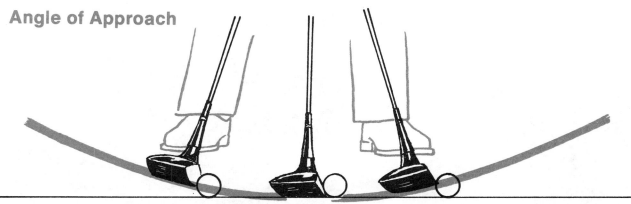

5   Because the ball rests below the player's shoulders, the club must swing downward and then upward again during the forward swing. It reaches the bottom of its arc for a brief span between the downswing and upswing. From a purely ballistic point of view, apart from any compensations by the player, the ball that is positioned well back in the stance will be struck relatively early in the forward swing, when the club's angle of approach is still somewhat downward. The ball positioned farther forward will be struck later in the swing, when the club's angle of approach to it is level or, perhaps, even upward.

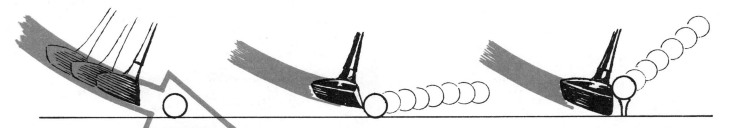

6   Shots struck early in the forward swing with the clubhead still moving on a steeply downward angle of approach will lose some length because the force of the blow is too much downward rather than forward (*left-hand illustration*). Often such shots will fly lower than normal because the downward angle of approach, in effect, reduces the loft of the club (*middle illustration*). However, the downward-moving clubhead may chop under a ball that is teed, catch it high on the clubface and thus lob it ineffectually upward (*right-hand illustration*).

7   Shots struck late in the forward swing, by which time the clubhead is moving on an upward angle of approach, may dribble along the ground because the club catches the top of the ball (*left-hand illustration*). Or the club may catch in the ground behind the ball, that being the lowest point in its arc (*middle illustration*). However, this is less likely to happen when the ball is teed (*right-hand drawing*), in which case a slightly upward angle of approach is ideal for driving the ball a long distance.

How Clubhead Path Affects Angle of Approach

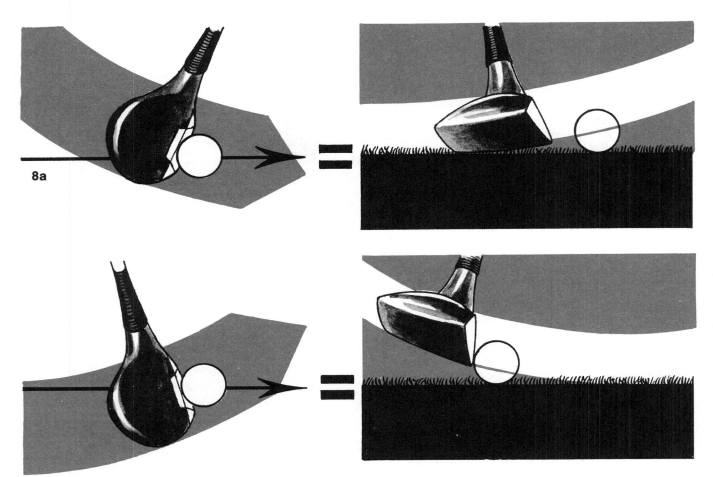

8a

8b

There is a direct relationship between the *path* on which the clubhead swings and its *angle of approach* into the ball. The more that the swing path is from the inside of the target line, the earlier the clubhead will reach the bottom of its arc. Thus the swing path back to the ball from well inside the line is more likely to produce a shallow or even upward angle of approach (*Illustration 8a*). The less that the path is from the inside, or the more it is from the outside, the later the clubhead will reach the bottom of its arc, and the more steeply downward its angle of approach will be (*Illustration 8b*).

well inside that line will have a relatively shallow angle of approach (*Illustration 8a*). The bottom of the swing arc will occur rather early. For this reason the clubhead may well hit the ground behind the ball or catch the ball on the upswing.

Thus players who swing to the ball on an extremely in-to-out path have trouble making solid contact when the ball is not teed. Indeed, they will automatically tend to tee the ball higher than normal. Also, they will especially enjoy playing on golf courses with fairways that are in first-class condition, so that the ball sits high atop the grass.

While the in-to-out swinger will tend to start his shots to the right of target—that being the direction in which the clubhead is moving—he will generally hit his long shots a good distance. This is true because the in-to-out swing path creates a shallow angle of approach which applies force forward rather than downward.

The opposite results begin to occur when the clubhead's path to the ball becomes less from the inside and more from outside the target line. The out-to-in path dictates that the angle of approach be more steeply downward (*Illustration 8b*). Usually impact occurs too early, before the clubhead has reached the bottom of its arc. Divots appear forward of the ball's original position. Distance decreases because of the downward direction of the blow. Shots tend to start left of target because the out-to-in path is in that direction.

The out-to-in swinger will unconsciously tend to tee his drives lower than normal, to avoid undercutting the ball with the downward chopping of the clubhead. He will, however, be less concerned about a ball that rests low in the grass or even on bare ground.

CLUBFACE ALIGNMENT

I have purposely explained clubhead path and angle of approach first and second in this chapter so that you can better understand and appreciate the *overriding* importance of clubface alignment.

Where your clubhead faces at impact is, as we shall see, the factor that invariably, in the long term, determines not only the path on which you will swing and your angle of approach, but also, to some extent, your clubhead speed.

The first thing to understand about the clubface's alignment at impact is that it can only be "closed," "open" or "square." The clubface is considered "closed" when it faces to the left of the direction it is moving. It is "open" when it faces to the right of its path. It is "square" if it faces in the same direction as it is moving (*Illustration 9*).

If the club faces squarely down its path of movement at impact, the ball will not only take off on that path but also continue straight in that direction, given on-centre contact without any influence of wind (*Illustration 9*).

If the clubhead is facing to the left of its path, the ball will curve to the left of that directional path. If it faces to the right of its path, the ball will curve to the right (*Illustration 9*).

In either case the degree of curve with a given club depends on the degree that the club faces to the left or right of its path at impact.

You will find, however, that your shots with a relatively straight-faced club, say a driver, will curve sideways more dramatically than will shots struck with a highly lofted club, such as a 9-iron or wedge, even if the clubface is misaligned to its path the same amount in each case.

This is true because the straighter-faced clubs apply less backspin to the ball than do the more-lofted clubs (*Illustration 10*). Because less backspin is present, any sidespin applied will tend to take over and dominate the shape of the shot.

Thus golfers who hit drives that start to the left and then curve to the right will invariably hit short approach shots that also start to the left but then continue in that direction on more or less a straight line (*Illustration 10*). In each case these players are making the same impact faults—an out-to-in clubhead path with the clubface open to that path—even though the shots themselves would seem to indicate differing impact conditions.

With this point in mind, I suggest that you rely on shots with your straighter-faced clubs to tell you if your clubface is misaligned to your swing path at impact. These shots will best reflect—by their sideways curve—any sidespin resulting from clubface misalignment.

Also, I suggest that you rely on shots with your more-lofted clubs—your 9-iron and wedge—to tell you the directional path on which your club is moving through impact. On these shots, with backspin dominating any sidespin, the ball will tend to fly in the same direction that the clubhead was moving.

The reason why I mentioned earlier that clubface alignment is more important than all other impact factors in the long term is that golf is a reaction game. The way we aim the club, position ourselves and, indeed, actually swing is usually an instinctive reaction to what the ball has done in the past. Here is a typical example showing how an error of clubface alignment at impact can, in fact, lead to instinctive reactions that cause further problems:

When they first start playing golf, most people have the innate

Clubface Alignment

9

Whereas the clubhead's path of movement at impact largely determines the direction in which a shot starts out, it is the alignment of the clubface in relation to that path that primarily determines the direction of any sideways curve thereafter.

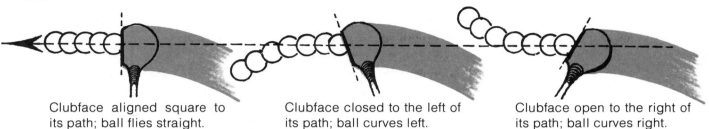

Clubface aligned square to its path; ball flies straight.

Clubface closed to the left of its path; ball curves left.

Clubface open to the right of its path; ball curves right.

10 Shots curve most dramatically with the relatively straight-faced, less-lofted clubs because they put less backspin on the ball. Thus any sidespin created by a misaligned clubface can take effect and make the ball curve sideways.

Shots curve less with the relatively slant-faced, more-lofted clubs because they put more backspin on the ball. This backspin tends to override the effect of sidespin so that the ball flies straighter.

11

The clubface, somewhat like the front of a swinging door, should align square to its path of movement throughout the swing. It should square to the target line for only the brief span when the path is on target. Attempts to align the face on target throughout the swing will often distort its alignment with the path at impact.

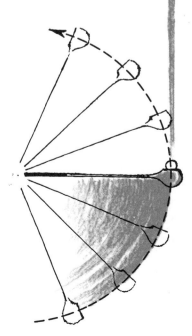

ability to aim the club on target. Most can also swing the club through impact more or less on line. Few, however, have the talent to square the clubface to that path at impact. Most of them find their long shots curving to the right, a result of the clubface being open to its path.

It will not be long before these golfers develop a fear of trouble on the right side of fairways and greens. They will react instinctively to this fear, and invariably their instinctive reaction will be incorrect. The most common such reaction is to simply aim the clubface to the left of target before swinging, to offset the expected curve to the right.

Unfortunately, aiming the clubface to the left automatically brings the handle end of the club too far back to the right, too far behind the ball, once the clubhead is soled flat on the ground. Since the golfer automatically positions himself according to where the club's handle happens to be, he too becomes positioned too far to the right of the ball. Thus by aiming the club to the left of target, the golfer, in effect, begins playing the ball too far forward in his stance.

Playing the ball too far forward to his left causes other automatic reactions. It forces the player to turn and align his shoulders too far to the left of target. It also forces him to grip the club with his hands turned too far to the left as well. Both of these reactions usually lead to even poorer shots.

With his hands turned too far to the left at address, the golfer has even more difficulty squaring his clubface to his swing path at impact. Thus his shots now curve even more sharply to the right. Aligning his shoulders to the left at address programmes the player to swing his club more to the left, on an out-to-in path, through impact. Since the out-to-in path all but guarantees a steeply downward angle of approach, with the force of the blow going more toward the ground rather than forward, the player also loses length on his shots.

With his shots now curving even more sharply to the right, this golfer will unconsciously aim his club even farther to the left. Thus the vicious cycle continues, at least until, finally, he somehow finds a correction that will allow him to square his clubface to its path at impact.

Once he achieves a square clubface at impact, the player's shots will still start out to the left, since his clubhead path is still out to in, but thereafter they will continue to fly in that direction with no curve to the right.

At this point the golfer's natural reactions to his shots will become correct reactions. He will tire of hitting shots to the left and, therefore, will begin to aim the clubface on target rather than to the left. This will bring the handle of the club, and thus the player himself, into proper relationship with the ball; it will no longer be too far forward in his stance. Proper ball position will lead to proper shoulder alignment and a correct grip, with both shoulders and hands turned less to the left.

In the end he will swing through impact on line with a proper angle of approach and with the clubface square to its path. His shots will start out pretty much on target, fly relatively straight and relatively far.

Once again, the purpose of this example is to stress the overriding importance of clubface alignment at impact. It was a clubface error—in this case its being open to the swing path—that caused all the wrong reactions. It was a squaring of the face to its path that led to correct reactions.

You will find it much easier to square your clubface to your clubhead path at impact if you will recall my earlier analogy of the swinging door. Once again visualize the door swinging, but this time liken your clubface to the front of the door. Like the door, it faces in a given direction before you start to swing (*Illustration 11*). It gradually faces more and more to the right of that direction during your backswing, just as the door faces more and more to the right as it opens. Like the door, the clubhead returns to its original position at impact. Then it faces more and more to the left thereafter.

Thus, throughout the swing the clubface remains square to its path of movement, though not to the target itself. It actually faces on target for only a brief span between downswing and follow-through, just as it swings on line for a similarly brief span. Again, this applies to all full shots.

Any attempt to make the clubhead face on target *throughout the swing* will only make it more difficult for you to coincide that facing with the clubhead's path of movement *at impact*.

CLUBHEAD SPEED   "What do you think determines how far a golf ball goes?"

This is often the first question I ask my students. It doesn't matter if I'm in England, America or wherever, there is always someone who answers, "Clubhead speed."

Thereupon I step forward and swing at a ball with all the clubhead speed that I can still muster.

The ball struggles upward and forward like a wounded bird into a headwind. Finally it plummets to earth not more than 120 yards from where I'm standing.

Maximum clubhead speed can give your shots maximum distance—but only if the impact conditions I've just explained are correct, so that all of that speed is applied squarely to the ball, not the ground or air around it.

There is a limit to the amount of clubhead speed a given individual can produce. Even the best golf instruction in the world cannot do much about that. Some people have more physical capacity to move the clubhead faster than others, just as some can run faster or jump higher.

While the capacity for hitting 300-yard drives is all too rare, it should, however, please you to know one thing that I have observed: of all the players I have met, the vast majority do have the physical capability to hit shots far enough to play the game much better than they do.

No, it is not a lack of physical capacity that causes most golfers to come up short on most holes. What does reduce their length is, first, the inability to transform that capacity into actual clubhead speed and, second, the inability to apply that speed correctly to the ball.

Actually, there is a direct relationship between generating your personal maximum clubhead speed and applying it squarely. The things that you do correctly to cause solid striking will also increase your clubhead speed. The things you do that cause your clubhead to mishit the ball are the same things that will reduce its speed.

For example, take the golfer who mishits shots because he returns the clubhead to the ball on an out-to-in path. Since his clubhead is moving toward the left of the target, he must somehow open his clubface to the right of its path to make the ball finish on target. Thus he must apply a glancing blow to the ball because his clubhead is moving in one direction and facing in another. Also, the blow must be additionally glancing because the out-to-in path causes the clubhead's angle of approach to be too steep.

The same leftward and downward clubhead path that led to the *misapplication* of this golfer's clubhead speed will also cause him to instinctively restrain himself in ways that actually *reduce* that clubhead speed. Sensing that he is swinging to the left and toward the ground, he will not clear his left hip to the left, nor will he swing his arms freely or release his hands—and thus the clubhead—freely into the shot.

Conversely, if this player were to swing on the correct path he would probably generate his maximum clubhead speed. With his club returning to the ball from the inside as it should, he would tend to clear his left hip to the left and release his arms and hands freely into the shot. He would sense that his shot would start out to the right if he did not do so.

ADDRESS POSITIONS INFLUENCE IMPACT FACTORS

Now, having explained at least the basic aspects of four impact factors, I would like to briefly point out something that you may have already noticed:

More often than not it is what you do *before* you swing that largely predetermines path, angle of approach, clubface alignment and clubhead speed at impact. How you grip the club, where you aim it, where you position yourself in relation to the ball, and how you align and posture yourself at address greatly influence *how* you swing, *what* your clubhead does to the ball and, thus, *how* your shots behave.

In my later explanations you will find, for instance, that your grip largely determines your clubface alignment at impact, that your body alignment at address can directly affect your clubhead's path, and that your posture before swinging largely determines its angle of approach.

Thus throughout this book I will stress correcting impact conditions, whenever possible, by merely changing what you do before you swing.

You will also find that in stressing preswing matters, I do not set forth one specific grip, ball position, body alignment or posture for all to follow. Rather, my instructions to you will be tailored to fit your own personal needs as determined by what your shots are doing.

I hope that at this point you are clear about the basic information I have presented in this section. If not, I strongly suggest that you restudy the preceding words and illustrations.

Once you fully comprehend this information, you will be well prepared to understand and apply the various diagnoses, explanations and corrections in the lessons that follow. Again, use the Contents and Lesson Guide to determine which of these lessons pertain to your particular shotmaking problems. Also, I hope that you will refer back to this opening section, if necessary, to further clarify the forthcoming instruction.

LESSONS TO CORRECT COMMON SHOT PROBLEMS

Lesson 1

Diagnosis: Shots with all clubs generally start out on target but shortly thereafter curve to the right, more so with the woods and longer irons, progressively less so as the loft of club increases. Your full shots tend to fly relatively high.

Explanation: The fact that your shots start on target tells me that your clubhead path is on line at impact, as it should be. However, their curving to the right thereafter indicates that your clubhead is "open," facing to the right of its path, at impact. The height of your shots further indicates the open clubface, which, in effect, increases the club's loft.

There are various causes of an open clubface at impact, but in my experience the most common of all is an incorrect grip. It is quite likely that you are setting your hands on the club so that they are positioned or turned too far to your left, and/or you are holding the club too tightly.

Regarding grip position, please bear this in mind: If before you swing, you face the club on target and hold it with a grip that allows you to see, say, one knuckle of your left hand, then you must return to that same one-knuckle position at impact for the clubhead to once again face on target (*Illustration 12a*). If you should return to a two- or three-knuckle position, your clubface will be facing to the right (*Illustration 12b*).

The expert male golfer who has played since childhood may have the strength and talent to return to a one-knuckle position at impact. However, most weekend players lack this capability. In trying to emulate the so-called weak grip position of the current hero, they merely assure themselves of playing numerous shots from trouble on the right. Far better it would be to copy the women professionals who, lacking the strength of their male counterparts, employ two- or three-knuckle grips. This makes it easier to return both hands and clubhead to their original pre-swing positions.

Regarding grip pressure, holding the club too tightly before swinging, or clenching it thereafter, tends to lock the wrists. As a result the clubhead trails the hands into the hitting area and thus arrives at the ball still facing the right.

Correction: Hold the club with both hands turned a little farther to your right, but not beyond the point that the V's formed between your thumbs and forefingers point to the tip of your right shoulder (*Illustration 12c*). If your shots still curve to the right, also lighten your grip pressure and maintain that lightness throughout

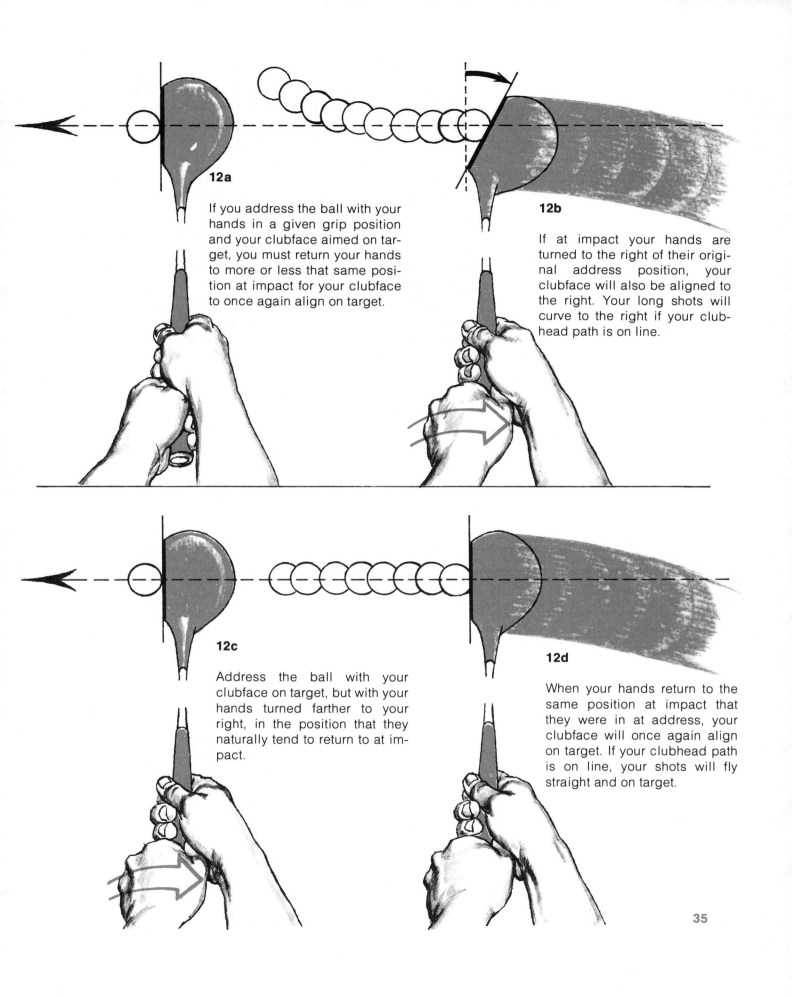

12a

If you address the ball with your hands in a given grip position and your clubface aimed on target, you must return your hands to more or less that same position at impact for your clubface to once again align on target.

12b

If at impact your hands are turned to the right of their original address position, your clubface will also be aligned to the right. Your long shots will curve to the right if your clubhead path is on line.

12c

Address the ball with your clubface on target, but with your hands turned farther to your right, in the position that they naturally tend to return to at impact.

12d

When your hands return to the same position at impact that they were in at address, your clubface will once again align on target. If your clubhead path is on line, your shots will fly straight and on target.

your swing. Any continued curving shots to the right after making these corrections will indicate that something other than your grip is causing the open clubface at impact. You should study other lessons in which the diagnosis mentions the curving of shots to the right.

Should your shots begin to curve left, you obviously will have turned your hands too far to the right and should reposition them less to the right.

Finally, bear in mind that a change of grip frequently feels uncomfortable for some time. Do not let this temporary discomfort lead to additional grip pressure. Above all, do not regress back to your former grip. As I explained in the preceding section, under Clubface Alignment, the resulting clubface error would, in time, lead to additional errors in aiming, ball positioning, body alignment, clubhead path and angle of approach.

Lesson 2

Diagnosis: Long shots generally start left and then slice to the right. The slice is most prominent with the longer clubs. Your full shots with the short irons tend to start left and continue in that direction with little or no curve to the right, as does the occasional shot with a longer, less-lofted club.

Explanation: Because we stand to the side of the ball we must swing the club forward on an in-to-in path. It must move *from* the inside—your side—of the target line during the downswing and then arc back *to* the inside during the follow-through (*see Illustration 2*). Thus it must be moving toward the right of target on the downswing and then left of target on the follow-through.

The fact that your shots start to the left indicates that your clubhead is not reaching the ball until it has already begun its return to the inside on the follow-through portion of its arc. The contact is too late in your swing. This late contact will occur if you are playing the ball too far forward, too far to the left, in relation to yourself (*see Illustration 3a*).

The fact that your long shots curve to the right is further indication of a forward ball position. As I explained in the section on impact factors, when shots curve to the right we naturally tend to start aiming the club to the left. Aiming left automatically sets the handle end of the club farther to the right, behind the ball, when the club is soled. Since we tend to position ourselves according to where the handle is, we thus place ourselves too far to the right of the ball as well. Thus the ball is too far left, or forward, and late contact is all but assured.

Moreover, with the ball forward we are forced to address it with our bodies, especially our shoulders, aligned too far to the left of target. This alignment makes us grip the club with our hands also turned too far to the left. This is a grip position that leaves the clubface open to the right of its path at impact (*see Lesson 1*) and thus reinforces the tendency to slice.

Correction: Play the ball farther back—less to the left—in your stance (*Illustration 13a*). This change of position might well need to be several inches.

As a result of this change, your shoulders will automatically want to align more to the right (*Illustration 13b*). Encourage this. Similarly, your hands will want to be turned farther to your right (clockwise) on the club (*Illustration 13c*). Again, make a conscious effort to let this happen.

From this new address position you should be able to see the

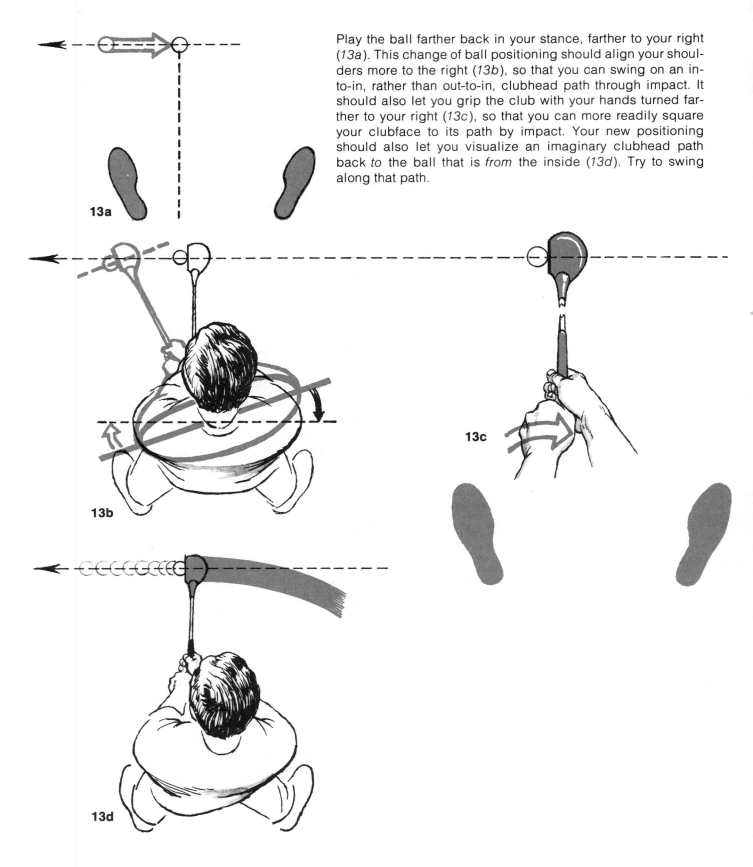

Play the ball farther back in your stance, farther to your right (*13a*). This change of ball positioning should align your shoulders more to the right (*13b*), so that you can swing on an in-to-in, rather than out-to-in, clubhead path through impact. It should also let you grip the club with your hands turned farther to your right (*13c*), so that you can more readily square your clubface to its path by impact. Your new positioning should also let you visualize an imaginary clubhead path back *to* the ball that is *from* the inside (*13d*). Try to swing along that path.

13a

13b

13c

13d

path along which your clubhead should return *to* the ball—that being a path that is *from* your side of the target line (*Illustration 13d*). See that path before you swing on every shot. Thereafter merely swing the club freely, up and down along that path, with your arms.

If your shots should begin to start out to the right of target, you will know that you have overcorrected and that your club is now reaching the ball too early in your swing. Simply set up to future shots with the ball a bit more to your left, until you find the position that sends it off toward your target.

If your shots should start out on target but still curve to the right thereafter, merely apply the grip corrections that I suggested in Lesson 1.

Lesson 3

Diagnosis: Your long shots have a general tendency to slice from left to right, and occasionally you chop under the ball and lob it upward—especially when it is teed—or top it along the ground to the left. Also, there is a general lack of distance, especially on your long shots.

Explanation: If your shots follow this pattern, I would wonder if perhaps at some time in your golfing career you had been warned against "casting" the club from the top of your backswing—"hitting from the top." Or perhaps you were encouraged to "lead with your legs" or hips in your downswing. Or maybe you have tried to emulate the famed "late-hit" position that we see in the photos of good players as they near impact with their wrists still cocked.

Such advice is fine for some. It *is* possible, and harmful, to uncock the wrists too soon. The legs and hips *do* have an important role to play. The late-hit position *is* ideal, if you also have the ability to square the clubface at impact.

However, almost any piece of golfing advice can cause trouble if carried to an extreme. In recent years the emphasis on using the legs and lower body, along with dire warnings against hitting from the top, has had just this effect on all too many players. Such advice has led to a general overuse of the legs and body and too little application of the arms and hands. Thus I find that most of my first-time pupils tend to swing *themselves* instead of the club.

The pattern of your shots tells me that you are one of these players. Your shots start left because your clubhead is moving across your target line in that direction, on an out-to-in path, at impact. Your long shots thereafter curve to the right because your clubhead is facing to the right of its path. You chop under tee shots and top other shots to the left because your club's angle of approach to the ball is too steeply downward, an inevitable result of swinging out to in (*see Illustration 8b*). Your lack of length on long shots indicates a relatively slow clubhead speed, apart from its obvious mishitting of the ball.

These problems of impact all result from the way you start your downswing. Instead of *swinging* the club freely with your arms and hands (*Illustration 14a*), you are *clinging* onto it with your hands while your legs and body unwind to the left (*Illustration 14b*). Unwinding while clinging instead of swinging forces your club to move outward before it can start downward; hence

14b

Swinging oneself instead of the club from the top of the backswing moves it toward the outside, rather than down from the inside, early in the downswing. Thus it moves into the ball on an out-to-in path that is also very steep. The clubhead lags behind and therefore remains aligned to the right of its path.

14a

Swinging the club freely with the arms from the top of the backswing moves it from the inside, where it was at the top, back to and along the target line. Doing so also helps square the clubface to the target by impact.

the out-to-in path and the resulting steepness of the angle of approach.

With the hands locked and without the arms swinging, neither can do their part in squaring the clubhead by impact. Instead it must lag too far behind the legs and hips and thus arrive at impact with its face still open to the right.

Swinging yourself instead of the club robs you of length because your clubhead cannot move at its own maximum speed. Instead, that potential becomes limited by its too-close association with your slower-moving body action.

Correction: Hit practice shots with your feet together, actually touching. Start with a 5-iron and the ball on a low tee. Remove the tee after you begin to make solid contact consistently.

As you hit these shots make sure that you initiate your downswing with your arms and hands. Even feel that you are casting the club, swinging it freely without overusing your body.

In your case this is not an incorrect feeling to cultivate. It will give you the free swinging of the arms and free release of the hands that all good players have developed naturally, almost without effort, early in their careers. You too must develop this free swinging if you are to ever transmit fully the power of your body to the clubhead and the ball.

Once you can feel yourself swinging the club freely with your arms and hands—you will no longer be falling off balance through overusing your body—then gradually widen the stance. If your old shot pattern returns, go back to this feet-together drill until you recapture this feeling.

Continue swinging your arms freely from the top of your swing even if your shots begin to curve in the opposite direction, from right to left. If the degree of curve becomes too severe, however, or if you tend to hit the ground behind the ball, combine a clearing or turning of your left hip to the left with your free arm-swing from the top.

Lesson 4

Diagnosis: Most long shots start out on target or to the right and then curve right thereafter. Occasionally, however, they hook sharply to the left instead. You often hit iron shots thin, taking no turf, or fat, taking turf behind the ball. You tend to lift your body or fall back onto your right foot during the downswing.

Explanation: I should remind you that we stand to the side of the ball. Thus the golf club must swing around our body as well as up and down and up again (*see Illustration 2*). It must arc to the inside as well as up on the backswing. It must arc back to the inside as well as up on the follow-through. Thus it must move on an in-to-in arc rather than a straight line.

The body must make room for the arms to swing freely on this in-to-in arc. It must do so by turning to the right on the backswing (*Illustration 15b*) and then clearing to the left on the forward swing (*Illustration 15c*).

When the body makes way for the arms to swing freely on this in-to-in arc, they can more readily square the clubface to the target line at the same instant that the clubhead returns to that line and the ball (*Illustration 15c*).

If the left side does not clear, however, the arms cannot square the clubface. They are blocked from doing so and the clubface often remains open, facing to the right, at impact. Shots curve in that direction. Occasionally the hands and wrists will react on their own, however; they will independently snap the clubface closed to the left prematurely so that the ball hooks sharply in that direction.

In either case, a failure to turn yourself to the right during your backswing, and the *resulting* inability to clear to the left on your forward swing, forces your arms to swing the club on more or less a straight line throughout. Thus the club moves too abruptly upward, downward and upward again. It is the abrupt upwardness of the throughswing—the upward angle of approach to the ball—that makes it all but impossible for you to take turf just after impact on your iron shots. Indeed, any turf that is taken is bound to be on the wrong side of the ball.

Your ability to turn away during your backswing and clear during your forward swing depends primarily on your posture at the ball before you swing. If your shots follow the pattern described in the diagnosis at the beginning of this lesson, I strongly suspect that you are bending your back and neck too far forward at address (*smaller illustration*). You may well be overdoing some previous advice to "keep your head down."

Good Posture Allows Turning and Clearing

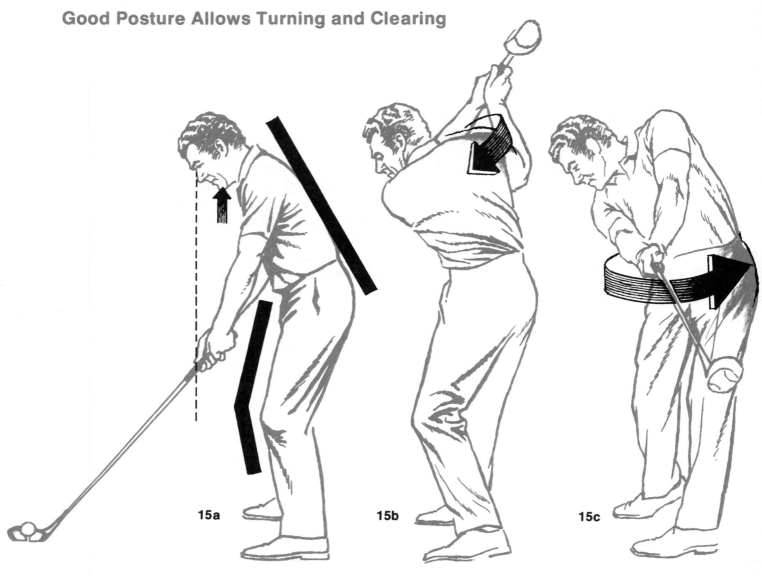

15a

15b

15c

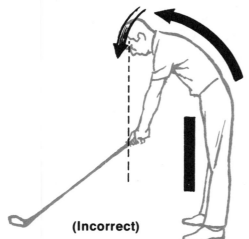

(Incorrect)

Proper posture at address—note knees flexed, back tilted forward only slightly from the hips, but not slouched, and chin up (15a)—makes it possible to *turn* your right shoulder away to the right as your arms swing back inside and up during the backswing (15b) rather than to *rock* and tilt it upward. Turning the right shoulder away instead of rocking it upward on the backswing allows your left side to clear to the left (15c), rather than slide and block, on the forward swing. With your left side cleared, your arms can swing freely down and forward on the desired in-to-in arc, thus "closing the door" and squaring the clubface by impact. The in-to-in path also provides a proper angle of approach for solid contact with the ball. Remember, however, that the whole sequence starts with proper posture at address.

This exaggerated head-over-the-ball position gives you the incorrect visual impression of the swing as being on a straight line. This impression would cause you to lift your right shoulder too much upward during your backswing, to rock it upward instead of turning it away to the right.

Failure to turn away on the backswing makes it difficult for your left hip to clear to the left on your forward swing. Thus rocking the shoulders going back leads to a blocking of the hips going forward. Since this blocking makes it difficult to shift your weight to the left, you fall back onto your right foot as your left leg and side stiffen and lift. You may, in fact, have reacted to this lifting by bending your neck and head even farther downward at address on succeeding shots, making certain to "keep your head down." This, of course, increases the rock-and-block tendency and makes turning and clearing even more unlikely.

Correction: Set up to the ball with your knees well flexed and your back more upright, not bent so far forward, so that a line extending straight down from your eyes would touch the ground closer to your toes and farther from the ball (*Illustration 15a*). Hold your chin up a bit higher as well.

An excellent way to develop this correct posture is by hitting practice shots from a sidehill slope where the ball is slightly higher than your feet.

From this address posture, merely turn your right shoulder away to the right—less upward than before—as you swing your arms back and up (*Illustration 15b*). This turning away with your right shoulder will allow your left hip to clear to the left as your arms swing the club from in to in during your forward swing (*Illustration 15c*).

With your shoulders now turning on a less upright plane, you may tend to top the ball on your first few shots. If so, continue with the instruction I have suggested, but also stress taking a divot by swinging your arms freely downward as you clear your left hip to the left. You may need to cultivate this free swinging of the club with your arms because the previous straight-line steepness of your swing had made such free swinging impossible without burying the clubhead into the ground.

Once you can combine the turning away and clearing through with a free swinging of your arms, your shots will begin to bore forward on a more penetrative trajectory for added distance.

Lesson 5

Diagnosis: Most long shots start out to the left, slice to the right thereafter and seem to lack much distance. Many short-iron shots pull to the left of the target with little or no slice. You may occasionally shank short iron shots off to the right.

Explanation: I should remind you that there are two elements to the backswing. One, the club must arc to the inside of the target line because we stand to the side of the ball. Two, it must also swing upward because the ball is sitting below our shoulders.

We achieve both of these elements through a combined turning of the right shoulder to the right—the hips also turn as a result—while swinging the club upward with the arms and hands.

Though this is a combined effort, it is the turning of the shoulders to the right that largely provides the inside element. It is the upward swinging of the arms and hands that primarily provides the upward element.

Illustration 16a shows the result of this combined effort at the top of the backswing. Notice particularly the separation between the relatively flat plane on which the shoulders have turned, to help provide the inside element, and the more upright plane on which the left arm has swung to help provide the upward element.

Without this separation of planes, without the arms swinging the club sufficiently upward as the body turns to the inside, it becomes very difficult to return the club to the ball on the proper path at maximum speed with the clubface squaring to the target line.

This is true because the start of the downswing tends to be a reaction to the finish of the backswing. If the club is on the inside and moving *upward* at the end of the backswing, as it should be, it will tend to swing *downward* from the inside in the downswing.

However, if the club finishes the backswing moving around to the *inside* but not *upward,* it will tend to swing back toward the *outside* instead of *downward* at the start of the downswing (*Illustration 16c*).

If your shot pattern fits the diagnosis at the start of this chapter, your backswing is probably lacking in its upward element. Your arms and hands are probably swinging the club on too flat a plane, a plane that is too closely allied with the plane of your shoulder turn (*Illustration 16c*). However, the reason for a flat backswing is invariably a faulty address position.

If one plays the ball too far forward (too far to the left in the

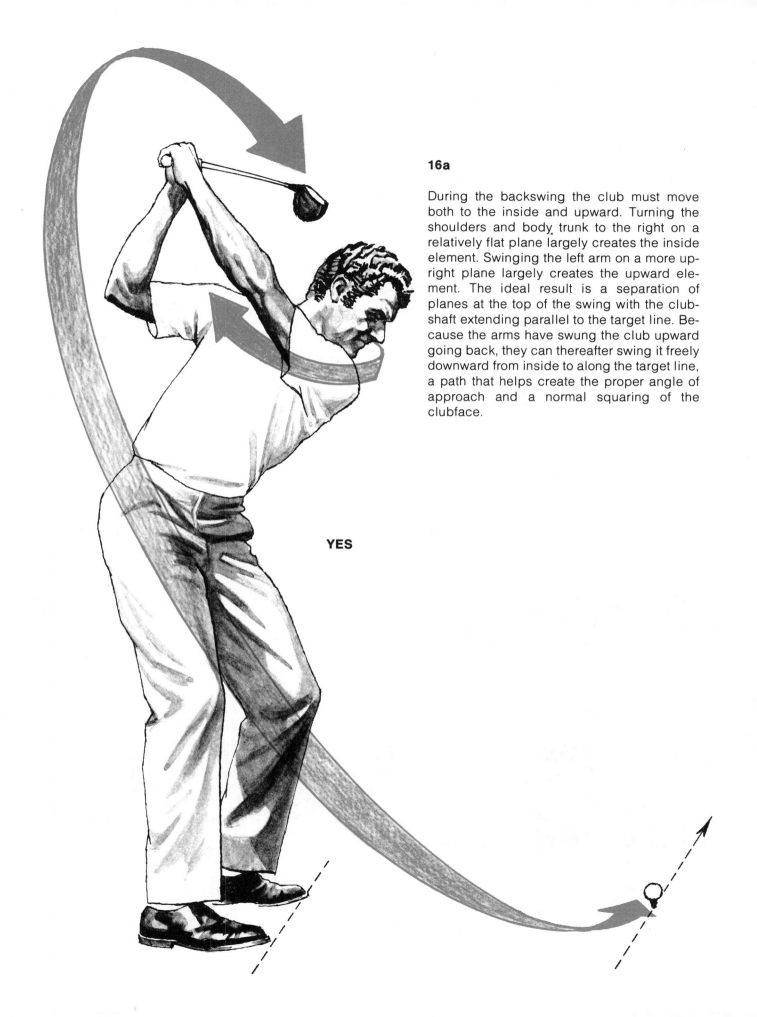

16a

During the backswing the club must move both to the inside and upward. Turning the shoulders and body trunk to the right on a relatively flat plane largely creates the inside element. Swinging the left arm on a more upright plane largely creates the upward element. The ideal result is a separation of planes at the top of the swing with the clubshaft extending parallel to the target line. Because the arms have swung the club upward going back, they can thereafter swing it freely downward from inside to along the target line, a path that helps create the proper angle of approach and a normal squaring of the clubface.

YES

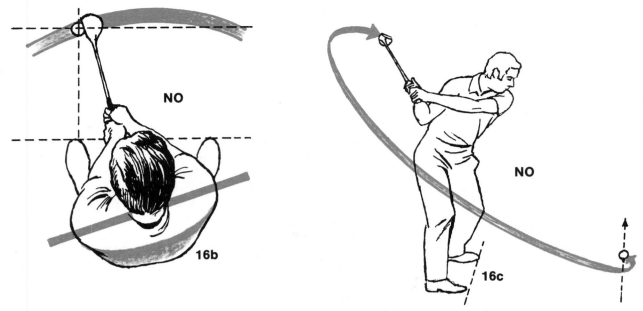

NO

NO

16b

16c

Playing the ball too far forward at address aligns the shoulders too far to the left. From this position, to swing the club sufficiently to the inside during the backswing, the arms must move around the body on a too-flat plane that is not sufficiently upward. Because they finish the backswing moving around to the inside rather than upward, they start the downswing moving around to the outside rather than downward. The result is an out-to-in path and an angle of approach that is too steep, which inhibits the squaring of the clubface.

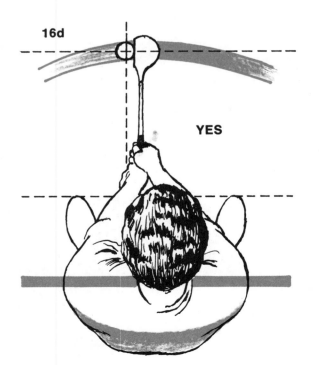

16d

YES

Playing the ball farther back in the stance automatically preturns the shoulders somewhat to the right before swinging. This helps provide the backswing's inside element and frees the player to focus merely on swinging the club freely upward and downward with his arms (as shown in *Illustration 16a*).

stance), the shoulders are forced to align too far to the left (*Illustration 16b*).

When the shoulders are aligned too far to the left, the arms cannot swing the club sufficiently upward without sacrificing the inside element of the backswing. Instead they must swing around on a flatter plane, along with a big turning of the shoulders and body, to move the club sufficiently inside the target line. Because the arms and hands swing around to the inside on a relatively flat plane, they also rotate clockwise to the right, thus fanning the clubface into an open position.

Because the backswing finishes with the club moving toward the inside rather than sufficiently upward, the downswing starts with it moving toward the outside rather than sufficiently downward (*Illustration 16c*). This results in the out-to-in clubhead path at impact that makes shots start out to the left. The outward swinging clubhead can also cause the occasional shank. The clubface is shoved out beyond the ball so that contact is made on the hosel (neck) of the club.

The slicing of long shots results because the left arm is swinging on a plane that is too similar to that of the shoulders. It cannot swing the club freely down to the ball from the inside and thus return the clubface back to square. Instead the face, which was fanned open during the backswing, remains open to the club's out-to-in path.

Lack of distance frequently occurs not only because of the glancing blow but also because the arms are being forced to swing at a relatively slow pace, one that is more akin to the slower-moving shoulders with which they are so closely allied in terms of plane.

Correction: Give yourself the inside element of your backswing before you actually swing. Do so by setting up to the shot with the ball played farther back to the right in your stance and your shoulders aligned farther to the right. Visualize a path running from the ball to the inside (*Illustration 16d*). Thereafter merely swing the club freely upward and downward along that path with your arms and hands. Let your body turn only as a *result* of swinging the club with your arms and hands.

If your shots continue to start out to the left, continue to apply this instruction but also practise with the feet-together drill suggested in Lesson 3. If your shots continue to slice to the right also apply the grip modifications suggested in Lesson 1.

If your shots begin starting out to the right, or if you begin taking divots behind the ball, combine a conscious clearing of your left hip to the left with the free swinging of your arms during your downswing.

Lesson 6

Diagnosis: Drives start out to the right of target and curve farther right thereafter. Shots with the shorter irons also push to the right but with little or no curve. Contact on iron shots tends to be either fat, with turf taken behind ball, or thin, with no turf taken at all.

Explanation: I would say that the shots just described are fairly prevalent among nearly good golfers. I see two or three players in this pattern every time I walk up and down the line at my golf centre. Occasionally you see the same pattern even among very good players.

The problem usually stems from a misconception that the path of the golf swing should be from in to out, with the clubhead moving toward the right of target at impact. With this idea in mind, the player makes such an effort to swing into the ball from the inside that he leaves his left hip in the way. His left leg and side stiffen and block, making it impossible for him to "close the door," so that the clubhead can return on line at impact (*see Illustration 2*) with the clubface squared to that path and that line as well (*see Illustration 11*).

As these illustrations clearly show, the ideal clubhead path through the hitting area is not in to out, but rather in to in. The clubhead should move *from* the inside, then briefly *along* the target line, and then back *to* the inside.

When the path is in to out instead, shots start out to the right because the clubhead is moving in that direction at impact. The blocking and stiffening of the left side that so often coincide with swinging in to out impede the arms from freely squaring the clubface; hence the open face at impact and the resulting curve to the right. Because the in-to-out path also causes a very shallow angle of approach, with the clubhead reaching the bottom of its arc relatively early (*see Illustration 8a*), contact is often made with the ground behind the ball (fat shots) or with the ball after the club has already started moving upward (thin shots). The tighter the lie of the ball in the grass, the more damning the in-to-out path becomes.

It is only natural that many golfers feel the swing should be in to out. At some stage of the downswing we all reach a "blackout" point, a time where everything is happening so fast that we lose recognition of what is actually taking place. Because this occurs during the downswing, when the club is, ideally, still moving from the inside, we tend to assume that it continues moving toward the outside after impact.

Clearing Left Hip Closes the Door

17

Clearing the left hip to the left brings the clubhead from inside to along the target line, rather than across that line from inside to outside. Clearing the hip also helps return the club square at impact. It is vital, however, that the arms and hands swing the club down as the hip clears.

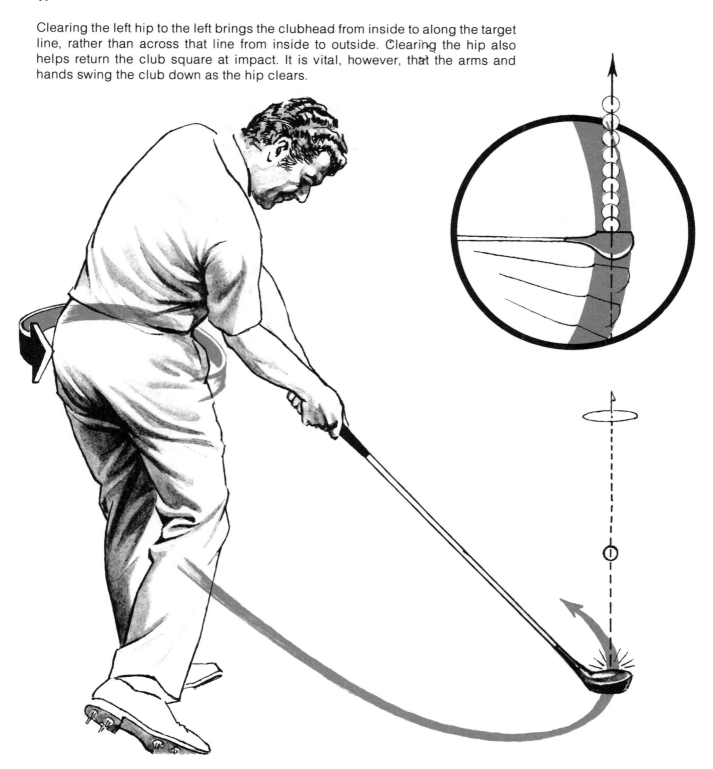

It is also natural that golfers who think "in to out" will fall into an additional trap when their long shots start bending to the right. These golfers may assume that slicing results from an *out-to-in* clubhead path, as, in fact, it often does. Naturally these players then make an even greater effort to swing even more from in to out. This makes "closing the door" even more difficult and further aggravates their problem.

Finally, golfers who think of the swing as being in to out also tend to play the ball too far back to the right in the stance. This rearward positioning of the ball allows them to align their shoulders to the right so that they can more readily swing from in to out. Unfortunately, with the ball too far back in the stance, the clubhead reaches it too early, when the clubface is still open and the path is in to out. The player has not had time to turn and clear his left hip to the left, which would bring the path from inside to straight and the face from open to square.

Correction: Bear in mind that the golf swing is in to in, not in to out. Set up with the ball a bit farther forward in your stance. Then make a conscious effort to turn and clear your left hip to the left early in your downswing. In other words, "close the door" so that at impact your swing path is from inside to on line, rather than in to out. The clubface, which is allied to the swing path, will thus square up at impact (*Illustration 17*).

If your shots should begin starting out to the left and, perhaps, curving to the right thereafter, you will know that you have begun to play the ball too far forward in your stance and/or failed to swing the club freely down and through with your arms and hands as you cleared your left hip. You should then consciously swing the club *down* as you clear the left hip.

Lesson 7

Diagnosis: Shots with all clubs generally start out on target but curve to the left thereafter. Shots with all clubs fly lower than normal. Your driver shots may fly so low that you have discarded this club in favour of a more-lofted wood or long iron.

Explanation: Your shots usually start out on target because your clubhead has returned to, and is moving along, your target line at impact. Good. They curve to the left, however, because your clubface is closed, facing to the left of your clubhead's path. They fly relatively low because the closed face, in effect, decreases the club's loft, thus making your driver, the least-lofted club, practically unplayable.

There are several factors that can contribute to a closed clubface at impact. The most common is an improper grip, the hands being incorrectly positioned and/or applying incorrect pressure to the club.

Regarding grip pressure, you may have read or been told that one way to avoid hooking shots to the left is to increase pressure with the last three fingers of the left hand. Or that a lighter right-hand grip will help eliminate early closing of the clubface.

I'm afraid I must disagree. Actually, the combination of a firm left hand and a light right hand, while fine for doing away with slicing, is likely to aggravate hooking. A tight left hand tends to slow the handle end of the club as it moves into the hitting area, thus allowing the clubhead to lash forward and close to the left prematurely. A soft right-hand grip causes the right wrist to be extremely supple and active, so that it too can contribute to the lash.

Regarding grip position, if you originally grip the club with your hands, say, turned well to your right (*Illustration 18a*), you will need to return to that same rightward positioning at impact for your clubface to once again be aligned on target. If you tend to reach impact with your hands turned farther to the left than their original rightward positioning (*Illustration 18b*), your clubface will invariably be closed to the left of its original facing. Thus, gripping with the hands turned too far to the right at address will tend to produce a clubface that has turned too far to the left by impact.

Correction: Hold the club with both hands turned a bit farther to your left, but not beyond the point that the V's formed between your thumbs and forefingers point to your chin (*Illustration 18c*). If your shots still curve to the left, make sure that the palm of your

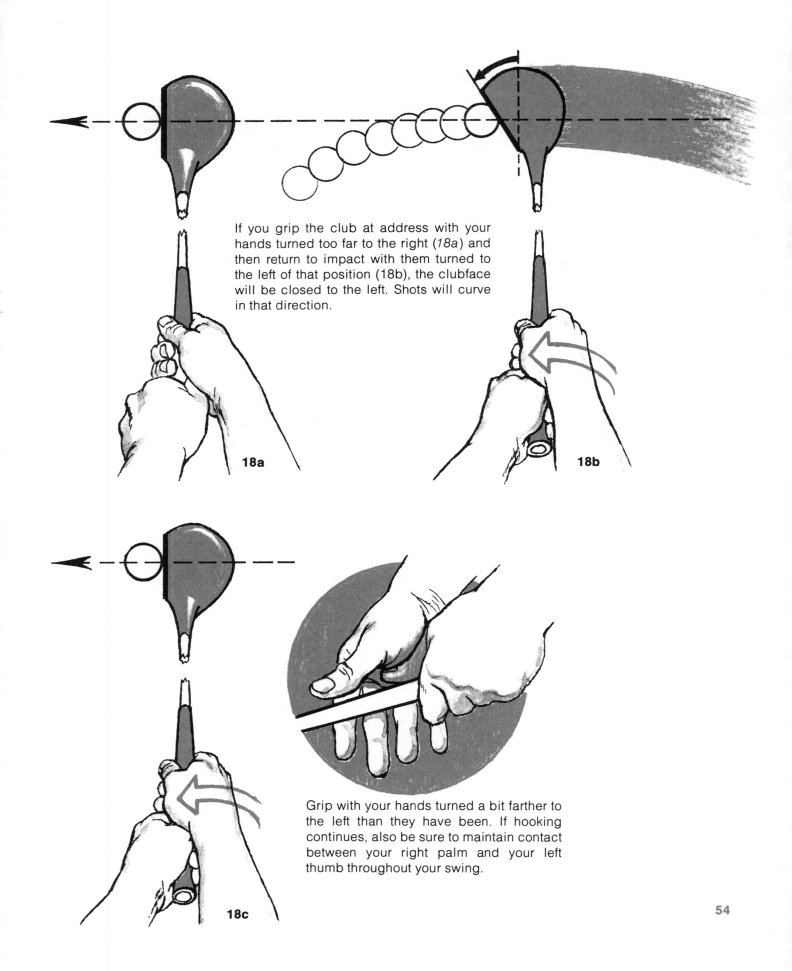

If you grip the club at address with your hands turned too far to the right (*18a*) and then return to impact with them turned to the left of that position (18b), the clubface will be closed to the left. Shots will curve in that direction.

18a

18b

Grip with your hands turned a bit farther to the left than they have been. If hooking continues, also be sure to maintain contact between your right palm and your left thumb throughout your swing.

18c

right hand stays firmly on top of your left thumb throughout the swing, but particularly at the top of your backswing. Any softening of the right hand at this stage creates backlash whereby the right hand and wrist become too active for the left hand and wrist to control. Any continued curving of shots to the left will indicate that something other than your grip is causing the closed clubface at impact. In that case you should study the other lessons that deal with hooking.

Should your shots start curving to the right, you will know that you have positioned your hands too far to the left and/or gripped too firmly with your right hand.

Lesson 8

Diagnosis: Long shots tend to start out to the right and then hook sharply to the left. Full shots with the more-lofted clubs also fly from right-to-left but with less curve. Shots with any club may occasionally start to the right and continue on that line without curving. Your drives may fail to get airborne, thus forcing you to use a more-lofted club on tee shots.

Explanation: Because we stand to the side of the ball, during the forward swing the clubhead must arc *from* the inside during the downswing and then back *to* the inside during the follow-through (*see Illustration 2*). Thus it will be moving toward the right of target on the downswing and back to the left of target during the follow-through. It will be moving on target for only a brief span between downswing and follow-through.

The fact that your shots usually start out to the right of target tells me that your contact with the ball occurs too early in your forward swing. Your clubhead is still moving to the right during the downswing portion or its arc, before it has had time to reach its on-target phase.

This early contact might well occur because you are playing the ball too far back (too far to the right) in your stance (*see Illustration 3b*). The fact that your shots generally curve to the left further indicates this possibility. Setting up with the ball too far to the right is typical of golfers whose shots have tended to finish to the left of fairways and greens.

These golfers invariably aim the club farther and farther to the right to offset the expected hook to the left. Aiming to the right, however, automatically sets the handle end of the club farther to the left, ahead of the ball, when the clubhead is soled. Since we tend to position ourselves according to where the handle is, these players automatically place themselves too far to the left of the ball. Thus the ball is too far right, or rearward. Early contact, with the clubhead still moving to the right, will occur unless the player somehow alters its path during his swing.

Moreover, with the ball positioned rearward the player is forced to turn his body, especially his shoulders, to the right as he addresses the ball. This alignment to the right also forces him to grip the club with his hands turned too far to the right. This is a grip position that tends to close the clubface to the left of its path by impact (*see Lesson 7*) and thus reinforces the tendency to hook.

Correction: Play the ball farther forward—more to the left—in your stance (*Illustration 19a*). This change of ball position will allow you to

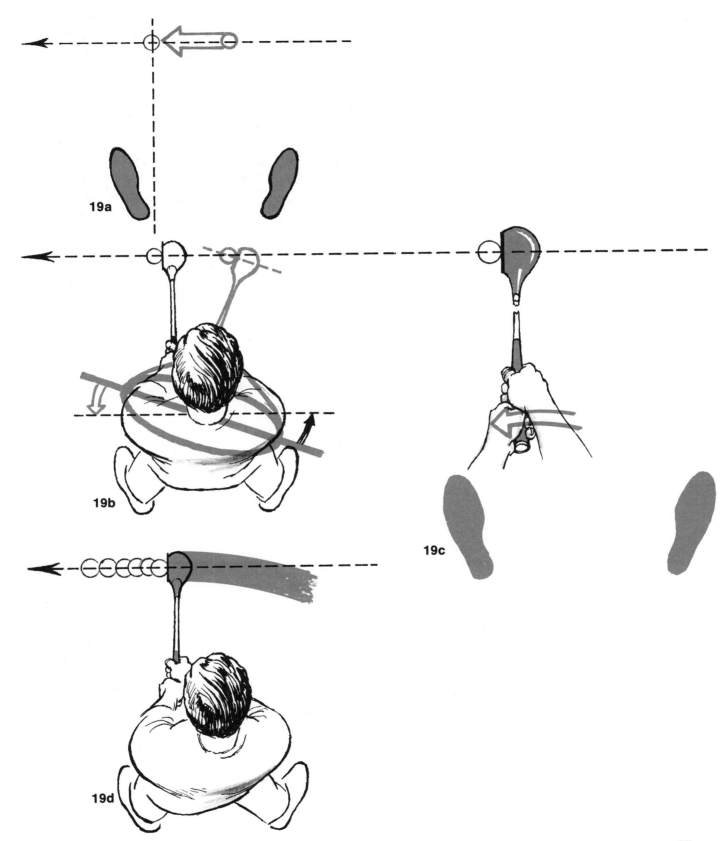

19a

19b

19c

19d

57

align your shoulders more to the left, as you should do (*Illustration 19b*). It will also allow you to turn your hands a bit more to the left when setting them on the club, as, again, you should do (*Illustration 19c*).

Your new address position should give you a somewhat different view of your target line as you address the ball. This line should appear to extend somewhat to the left of where it had been (*Illustration 19d*). Keep this new target line in mind and try to swing the clubhead along it through the impact area.

If your shots should begin to start out to the left of target, you will know that you have positioned the ball too far to the left, so that your club is reaching it too late in your swing, by which time it has already started arcing back to the inside. Merely address future shots with the ball a bit less to the left until you find the positioning that starts your shots off toward your target.

If your shots should start out on target but still curve to the left thereafter, merely apply the grip corrections that I suggested in Lesson 7.

Lesson 9

Diagnosis: Shots start out to the right and then hook to the left. Lack of distance is not your problem, but frequently you either take turf behind the ball or top the shot along the ground to the right.

Explanation: Ideally we would like impact to take place at that brief instant when

—Our clubhead is moving along the target line, "on-line," just after it has moved from the inside and just before it has returned back to the inside

—Our clubface is aligned square to that on-line path

—Our clubhead is at the bottom of its downward-upward arc

For impact to occur at this instant, a certain element of "timing" is required in the downswing. To me, proper timing is nothing more than coordinating leg and hip action with swinging the arms. As the left hip turns and clears to the left, the arms should swing the club freely down and forward, back to the ball from inside to along the target line.

Improper timing occurs when leg and hip action does not coordinate with swinging the arms, or vice versa. If the lower half of the body turns before the arms swing, the club lags behind. At impact the blade still faces to the right while moving to the left—out to in—because of the early turning in that direction. This was the problem of the player that I described in Lesson 3, the slicer who delayed his arm swing for fear of casting or hitting from the top.

Yours is the opposite problem, however. If your shots fit the pattern described here, you are probably, indeed, casting the club with your hands and wrists at the start of your downswing. The club is too quick for your hip and leg action.

Because your hands and arms are so active so soon in your downswing, your clubhead reaches the bottom of its arc too soon, before it gets to the ball (*Illustration 20a*). That explains why you frequently take a divot behind the ball or catch the ball on your upswing and thus top it along the ground.

Your shots tend to start out to the right because your clubhead is still moving in that direction, from the inside, at impact. It has not yet reached the on-line portion of its arc because your hip action has been left behind.

Your shots thereafter curve to the left because your hands and arms, again being too active too soon, have closed the clubface to the left of its path by impact (*Illustration 20a*).

I have found that the tendency to cast or throw the club with

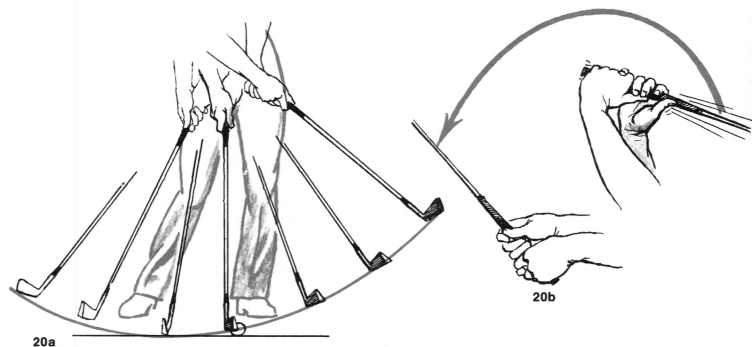

20a

20b

When the hands and wrists cast the clubhead into the hitting area before the left hip clears to the left (*20a*), the club reaches the bottom of its arc behind the ball and then starts upward. Fat or topped shots result. Also, the clubface closes to the left prematurely because of the casting (*20a*). Separation between the hands at the top of the backswing (*20b*), and the subsequent reconnection during the downswing, often are the cause of the casting.

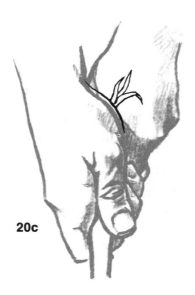

20c

20d

To cure these problems, practise with a blade of grass placed between the top of your left thumb and your right palm (*20c*). Apply enough pressure to hold the grass in place throughout your swing while also making sure to clear your left hip to the left during your downswing (*20d*).

the hands from the top of the swing occurs because the hands have not remained firmly together. The left thumb and the right palm have separated during the backswing and then reconnected at the start of the downswing. This reconnection forces the wrists to uncock prematurely (*Illustration 20b*).

Correction: When practising, place a blade of grass along the top of your left thumb and make sure that your right palm holds it firmly in place throughout your swing (*Illustration 20c*). This will eliminate the separation between your hands that has caused you to cast the club and thus close its face to the left of its path. With casting eliminated, your shots will no longer curve to the left.

They will, however, continue to start out to the right until your clubhead swings on line, rather than in to out, at impact. To make it swing on line at impact, start your downswing by consciously turning your left hip to the left as you swing the club with your arms. Clearing this hip to the left (*Illustration 20d*) not only will bring your clubhead's path on line but will also cause the bottom of your swing arc to coincide with the ball, rather than some spot behind it.

Lesson 10

Diagnosis: Your shots fly too low, too flat. Most hook from right to left or from on line to the left. Some push out to the right, flying low with little or no curve. Your best shots are those played off a tee or from a good lie on the fairway. You seldom, if ever, use a driver, but you do well driving with a 3-wood or 4-wood. Your worst shots are from normal or tight lies where you take turf too early, behind the ball, or not at all.

Explanation: The correct path of the golf swing is from in to in. The club moves to inside the target line during the backswing, then back to the line during the downswing and then back to the inside during the follow-through.

This in-to-in aspect of the swing should result primarily from turning the body to the right during the backswing and then clearing the left hip to the left during the forward swing.

There is also, however, an upward-downward-upward element to the swing. The club must move upward during the backswing, downward during the downswing and then upward again during the follow-through as it swings on the in-to-in path.

The upward-downward-upward element should result primarily from the arms swinging the club up, down and then up again as the body turns.

Golfers whose shots follow the pattern described in the diagnosis do, in fact, turn and clear very well. Thus they do achieve the in-to-in clubhead path.

At the same time, however, they fail to swing the arms sufficiently upward, downward and upward again. The arms swing on a plane that is too similar to the relatively flat planes on which the shoulders turn away to the right and the hips clear to the left. Thus the club swings on an arc that is too flat.

It also swings on a path that is too far to the inside during the backswing and too quickly to the inside during the through-swing. Because the swing is too flat and too much in to in, the arms and hands tend to close the clubface to the left too quickly in the hitting area. Thus most shots curve to the left. The closed face also "delofts" the club. The relatively straight-faced driver, when delofted, often fails to get the ball into the air at all.

Also, because the swing is too flat and too much from the inside, the clubhead moves into the hitting area on a very shallow, almost level, angle of approach. Unless the ball is teed or sitting high on the grass, the shallow-swinging clubhead tends to catch turf behind the ball or to contact the ball's upper portion

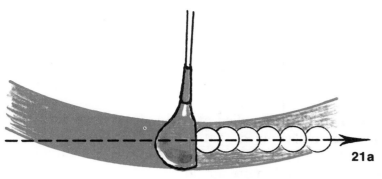

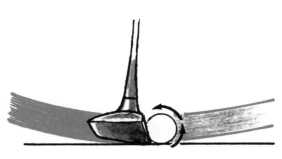

21a

When the swing plane is correct, the clubhead returns to the target line from *slightly* inside it. The clubface remains square to that path and thus *gradually* squares to the target line. The clubhead returns to ball level on the correct angle of approach.

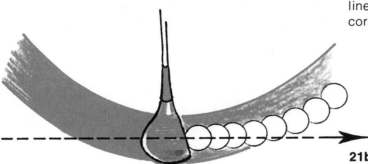

21b

When the swing plane is too flat, the clubhead returns to the target line from *too far* inside, causing shots to start out to the right. The clubface often closes abruptly to the left of that path, causing the shot to curve left. The angle of approach is so shallow that clean contact is difficult unless the ball is teed or sitting high on the grass.

21c

Hitting practice shots with your backside close up to an object such as a bush or hedge will eliminate a flat swing plane. Make your normal shoulder turn but swing your arms on a more upright plane to avoid hitting the object with your club.

while moving upward. Fat or thin shots from the fairway are all too common.

Correction: Hit practice shots while standing backed up to a large bush or hedge, or some similar object that will not damage your club (*Illustration 21c*). As you swing, make your normal body turn but swing your arms on a more upright plane, so that your club will avoid the object that is behind you.

The very good golfer might also hit practice shots off bare hard ground with a driver. He will quickly sense that he can contact the ball, rather than the ground behind it, only by swinging the club more upward and then downward on a steeper angle of approach.

Lesson 11

Diagnosis: Shots generally fly rather high. They usually start to the right of target then either continue to the right with little or no curve or, frequently, hook to the left. Your left leg and side often feel stiffened or blocked during and after impact. Lack of distance is not your problem.

Explanation: This particular shot pattern is more common among better golfers (including many professionals) who at some stage frequently hooked the ball into trouble on the left. To avoid this problem they will have made certain address position and swing adjustments, either instinctively or consciously. The more instinctive adjustments might have included

—Aiming the club and aligning the body to the right of target at address (to offset the expected hook to the left)

—Sliding the legs and lower body laterally to the left at the start of the downswing, with relatively little turning and clearing of the left hip to the left (which, again, is the side of the golf course that they had learned to fear)

—Swinging the club back to the ball from well inside the target line (again, to avoid trouble on the left)

Some of the more conscious adjustments to avoid hooking might have included

—An effort to swing on a more upright plane (if the player had heard or sensed that a flat swing causes hooking, as indeed it can [*Lesson 10*], or if he had felt or heard that a more upright, on-line swing would improve his accuracy, since that—rather than distance—is his particular worry)

—An effort to bend well forward from the hips at address (to allow a more upright swing)

—An effort to start the clubhead back straight along the target line during the takeaway (again, to produce a more upright swing)

The end result of these well-meaning efforts is all too often a swing in which the left hip cannot turn and clear to the left during the forward swing (*see Illustration 17*). This clearing of the left hip to the left helps contribute length to shots but, more importantly, is vital for consistent accuracy.

When the left hip clears to the left, the arms can *gradually* turn the clubface counterclockwise from open to closed, throughout the entire forward swing. Because it turns gradually over such a long span, the chances of the face being square at impact are relatively good.

When the left hip does not clear to the left, however, this natural and gradual turning is thwarted. The left side blocks the arms from swinging freely forward through the hitting area. The clubhead keeps moving forward, however, and thus the clubface closes abruptly to the left (see Illustration 20a).

If the clubface turns to the left the slightest instant before impact, the shot will start out to the right—that being the in-to-out path of the golfer who fears hooking to the left—and thereafter curve to the left. If contact occurs a bit earlier, before the clubface has closed to its path, the shot will push out to the right and continue in more or less that direction.

While failing to fully clear the left hip to the left is a natural tendency among golfers who fear hooking the ball in that direction, such clearing can become all but impossible if they try to end hooking by swinging more upright.

This is true because clearing the left hip to the *left* on the forward swing depends largely on turning one's right shoulder and side to the *right* during the backswing. If efforts to swing more upright lead to rocking the right shoulder and side more upward and less around to the inside during the backswing, these efforts will, in the end, cause more lifting and more blocking with the left side during the forward swing. Thus, trying to improve accuracy through swinging more upright can, in fact, actually reduce accuracy by making the necessary clearing of the left hip all too difficult.

I should add that the tendency to rock and block, rather than turn and clear, is quite common among golfers who aim the club and align themselves too far to the right at address, as hookers tend to do to offset the expected curve of the ball to the left.

The player who aligns to the right often senses that he has, in effect, already preturned to the right to some extent before swinging. Thus he fails to turn his right side sufficiently during his backswing, but rocks it upward instead.

Correction: First give yourself a grip that will make hooking impossible, thus eliminating any fear of trouble on the left. Merely set your hands on the club turned a bit farther to the left (see Illustration 18c) and hold tighter with your right hand. (Lesson 7 explains why this grip eliminates hooking.) With fear of the left eliminated, you should feel free to clear your left hip to the left during your downswing as you swing the club freely down and through with your arms.

To make this clearing to the left possible on the downswing, during your backswing you will need to turn your right shoulder to the right—less upward than before—as you continue to swing the club upward with your arms (*see Illustration 15b*).

To turn your shoulders on a less upright plane, set up to the ball in a more upright posture, with your knees well flexed and with less forward bending at the hips and neck (*see Illustration 15a*).

Lesson 12

Impact feels solid, but the ball flies left of target with little or no curve. You may feel the need to make a large body turn during the backswing. Shanking iron shots to the right may also be a problem.

Explanation: This diagnosis indicates the tendency to pull shots to the left. Contact feels solid because at impact the clubface is aligned square to the clubhead's path. The ball flies to the left, however, because the clubhead is moving in that direction (*Illustration 22a*).

I have found that golfers who frequently pull shots to the left on more or less a straight line are often ex-slicers whose long shots at one time had curved to the right. Their shots no longer slice because they have learned to square the clubface to its path at impact. As yet, however, they have not corrected the path to the left that so often evolves from slicing to the right.

As slicers, these golfers began aiming the club to the left at address to offset the curve to the right that they had come to expect. Aiming to the left brought the handle end of the club too far to the right, behind the ball, when the clubhead was soled. This automatically forced these golfers to stand too far to the right of the ball or, in effect, to play the ball too far to the left, too far forward, in the stance.

With the ball too far forward, the clubhead could not reach it during the forward swing until the clubhead had already begun moving back to the inside—to the left of target—on the follow-through portion of its arc (*Illustration 22a*).

Playing the ball too far forward also forces golfers to align the shoulders and body too far to the left at address (*see Illustration 16b*). This type of shoulder setup often leads to an unusually large shoulder turn during the backswing in an effort to get the club to the inside of the target line. Frequently, in fact, these golfers are encouraged to increase their backswing pivot.

Exaggerating the shoulder turn to the inside during the backswing will cause them to overturn to the outside at the start of the downswing, resulting in an out-to-in clubhead path at impact (*see Illustration 16c*). It also causes shanking, since the overturn to the outside pushes the clubhead outward, leading to contact being made on the hosel or neck of the club.

Correction: Play the ball farther back, farther to the right, in your stance (*Illustration 22b*). This will cause your clubhead to reach it sooner in your forward swing, while it is still moving on line to

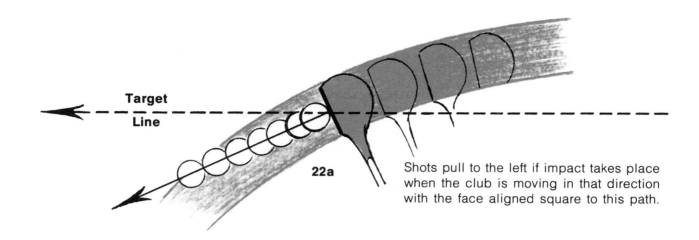

Target Line

22a

Shots pull to the left if impact takes place when the club is moving in that direction with the face aligned square to this path.

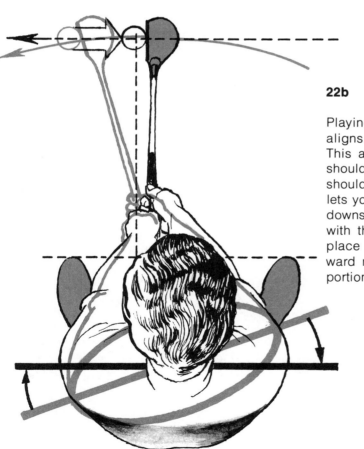

22b

Playing the ball farther back to the right in the stance aligns the shoulders correctly, rather than too far left. This alignment eliminates the need for the excess shoulder action on the backswing that causes the shoulder-dominated, out-to-in forward swing. It also lets you visualize beforehand the proper backswing-downswing path on which you should swing. Finally, with the ball played farther back, impact will take place earlier, before the clubhead has begun its leftward movement to the inside on the follow-through portion of its arc.

your target, before it has had a chance to return back to the inside and thus be moving to the left.

Playing the ball back will help you to align your shoulders correctly (*Illustration 22b*) and thus will eliminate any need to overpivot during your backswing.

The new ball position and shoulder alignment will also allow you to visualize, at address, the path on which you should swing the clubhead. Visualize the path—a few feet will do—running from the ball back to the inside of the target line. Thereafter merely swing the club freely up and down with your arms so that the clubhead moves up and down this predetermined path.

Hit practice shots until you find the specific ball position and related shoulder alignment that allow your shots to start out on target. If it should happen that they curve to the right of target thereafter, do not change your ball position or shoulder alignment. Instead, merely grip the club with your hands turned a slight bit farther to the right. This grip adjustment will make it easier for you to square your clubface to the clubhead's new on-line path at impact.

Lesson 13

Diagnosis: Impact feels solid, but the ball flies right of target with little or no curve. Your left side may feel as if it is in the way of your forward swing.

Explanation: The golfer whose current bad shot is a push to the right of target is often someone who in the recent past had tended to hook shots to the left of target. Now his shots rarely curve left because he has corrected the problem that was causing his clubface to align to the left of the clubhead's path at impact. There probably has been an unconscious grip change which corrected this clubface error.

Since he has learned to square his clubface to his swing path, he now makes the fairly solid contact with the ball. His shots fly to the right, however, because his clubhead is still moving in that direction when it reaches the ball (*Illustration 23a*).

As I explained in the section on impact factors, since we stand to the side of the ball we must swing the clubhead along an arc, rather than a straight-line path. During the forward swing the clubhead arcs from inside the target line to along that line, briefly, and then back to the inside, much like a swinging door gradually closes from right to left (*see Illustration 2*).

If impact occurs too early in the forward swing, before the door has closed, the clubhead will still be moving from the inside and, thus, toward the right of target (*see Illustration 3b*).

Such is the case of the ex-hooker who now pushes shots to the right. Having seen his shots frequently curve into trouble on the left, he instinctively began to aim his club and align his body to the right. Aiming and aligning to the right forced him to play the ball too far back in his stance, too far to his right. It is this rearward positioning of the ball that still causes his clubhead to reach it too early in the forward swing, while still moving to the right on an in-to-out path, before he has had time to "close the door."

Moreover, I have found that many golfers who aim and align to the right tend to make a backswing turn that is too steep. Aligning to the right at address preturns these players to the inside to a certain extent before they swing. Therefore, rather than turn the right shoulder farther to the inside during the backswing, they tend to merely rock or lift it upward instead.

The normal reaction to this upward rocking of the right side during the backswing is an extreme lifting of the left hip during the forward swing. When the left side lifts, it cannot turn and clear to the left as it should. It blocks the forward swing. The

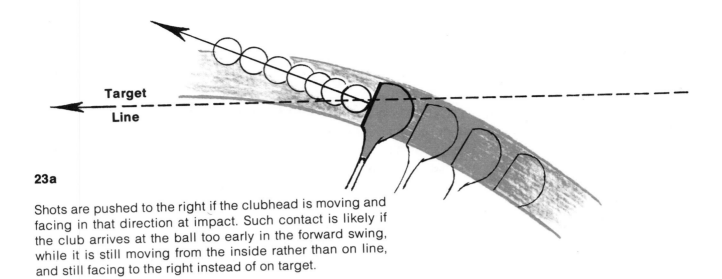

Target Line

23a

Shots are pushed to the right if the clubhead is moving and facing in that direction at impact. Such contact is likely if the club arrives at the ball too early in the forward swing, while it is still moving from the inside rather than on line, and still facing to the right instead of on target.

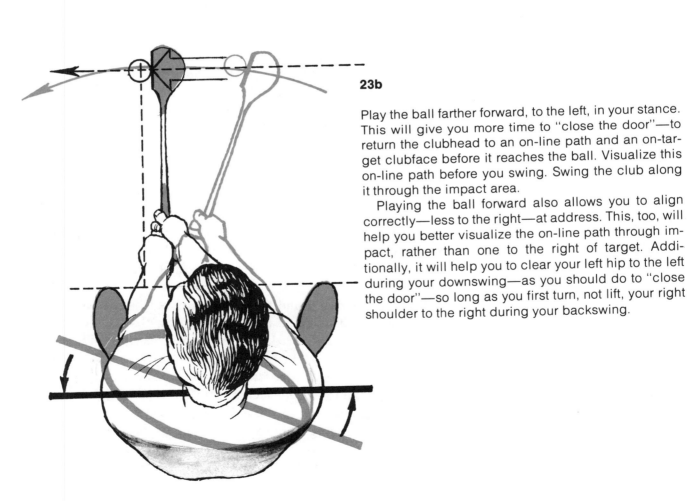

23b

Play the ball farther forward, to the left, in your stance. This will give you more time to "close the door"—to return the clubhead to an on-line path and an on-target clubface before it reaches the ball. Visualize this on-line path before you swing. Swing the club along it through the impact area.

Playing the ball forward also allows you to align correctly—less to the right—at address. This, too, will help you better visualize the on-line path through impact, rather than one to the right of target. Additionally, it will help you to clear your left hip to the left during your downswing—as you should do to "close the door"—so long as you first turn, not lift, your right shoulder to the right during your backswing.

door fails to close. Thus golfers who push shots to the right often feel that their left side is in their way at impact and during the follow-through.

Correction: Play the ball farther forward, farther to the left in your stance (*Illustration 23b*). This will allow a bit more time for your clubhead to return to an on-target path by impact. It will give you more time to close the door. Thus your shots will begin to start out on target.

Playing the ball farther left will also allow you to align your shoulders more to the left at address (*Illustration 23b*). I would hope that this new alignment will encourage you to turn, rather than lift, your right shoulder during your backswing (*see Illustration 15b*). As I have explained, turning rather than lifting on the backswing will allow you to turn and clear your left hip to the left during your downswing. This, too, will help close the door and return your clubhead to the ball during the on-line portion of the forward swing.

It will help if you visualize this on-line path running through the ball before you swing (*Illustration 23b*). Thereafter, as you return to impact with your left hip clearing, try to swing the clubhead freely down that path with your arms.

To summarize: Before swinging, ball forward, align left, visualize an on-line path running through the ball. While swinging, turn right shoulder away on backswing, clear left hip to the left on downswing as arms swing club freely through impact on the path you have visualized.

I suggest you hit some practice shots until you find the specific ball position and related shoulder alignment that start your shots out on target. If they should happen to curve to the left thereafter, do not change your ball positioning or alignment. Instead, merely grip the club with your hands turned a bit farther to the left. This grip adjustment will allow you to once again square the clubface to your clubhead's new, on-line path at impact.

Lesson 14

Diagnosis: Many shots are topped along the ground, often to the left but not consistently so.

Explanation: This particular shot pattern is common to the beginning golfer. He can't do the one thing he wants to do most, which is simply to make the ball go into the air.

He fails because his clubhead doesn't return to the bottom of the ball to send it upward. Instead, contact is made high on the ball, if at all, which drives it downward along the ground.

You should understand that in assuming the address position before swinging, we establish a certain distance between ourselves and the bottom of the ball. We measure this distance with our left arm and the golf club as we set it on the ground just behind the ball. The arm and club combine to form a certain radius for the swing (*Illustration 24a*).

During the backswing we "lose" a large part of this radius because the wrists cock (*Illustration 24b*).

During the downswing the wrists should uncock fully to reestablish the original radius (*Illustration 24c*). If they do not, the clubhead does not get back to the bottom of the ball (*Illustration 24d*).

While the downswing should combine free arm and hand action (swinging the club) with leg and body movement (swinging oneself), it is the arm and hand action that primarily uncocks the wrists and reestablishes the radius (*Illustration 24c*). Too much leg and body movement and too little free-swinging of the golf club delay the uncocking.

Many good golfers do stress leg and body action, but only because they mastered swinging the club freely with the arms and hands long ago. Many, if not most, beginners and poorer golfers more or less swing themselves rather than the club.

Reestablishing the swing radius by impact, which requires swinging the club freely with the arms and hands throughout the forward swing, should be the beginning golfer's first priority.

Correction: Address the ball as you normally do, but then pick out a spot two or three inches behind it. Try to take some grass with your clubhead at that spot during your forward swing.

This practice technique will automatically put more arm and hand action into your downswing, and thus help you reestablish your radius by impact. Continue to play shots this way until you begin to consistently take turf behind the ball. Then you should begin to focus on the ball itself, rather than the spot behind it.

24a

24b

24c

24d

Incorrect

Lesson 15

Diagnosis: You frequently top shots along the ground to the left of your target line. The long shots that you do not top also start out to the left, but thereafter slice to the right. They fly a short distance on a low trajectory.

Explanation: It is not uncommon to combine topping to the left with slicing from left to right. In each case, shots start left because the clubhead is moving in that direction, on an out-to-in path, at impact.

Correction: They run along the ground or, at best, fly somewhat low because the clubhead chops down into the top or back of the ball at a steeply downward angle of approach. As I have mentioned, the out-to-in clubhead path forces this angle to be too steep (*see Illustration 8b*).

When the club's path is out to in and steep, contact invariably occurs too early, before the clubhead reaches the bottom of its downswing-upswing arc (*see Illustration 8b*). Thus golfers who top shots to the left seldom take a divot behind the ball. They usually slice their better long shots, however, because this type of impact has not allowed the clubface enough time to square to its path. Thus it reaches the ball while still facing to the right.

All of these impact faults can be caused by a single swing error that takes place at the start of the downswing. At that point the golfer has three choices. He can either (a) swing himself—his legs and body—with no accompanying hand and arm action or (b) swing the club with his arms and hands but independent of any body action or (c) combine hip-and-leg movement with arm-and-hand action.

Of these three choices, the last is best. Swinging the club with the hands and arms starts it back to the ball from inside the target line, where it was at the top of the backswing (*see Illustration 14a*). Simultaneously clearing the left hip to the left not only allows room for the arms to swing through, but also brings the clubhead back to an on-line path at impact and squares the clubface to that path.

The golfer who combines topping shots to the left with slicing from left to right is one who swings himself but leaves out swinging the golf club. He turns to the left at the start of his downswing but fails to start the club back to the ball as well. He clings to it with his hands but fails to swing it downward from the inside with his arms and hands (*see Illustration 14b*).

By the time his club can finally start downward, his body has already turned to the left. This moves the club outward toward

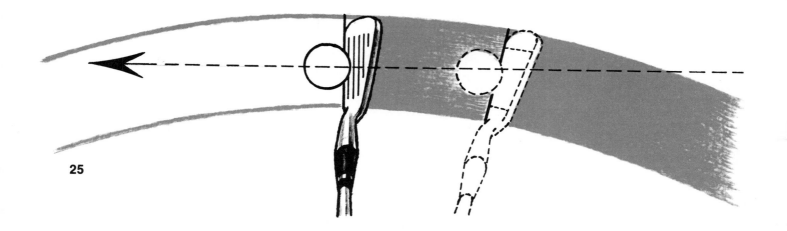

25

the target line instead of downward toward the ball. Thereafter it can only swing steeply downward on an out-to-in path.

Address the ball making sure you can see a path running from the ball back to the inside (*Illustration 25*). Imagine that the ball is sitting on that line an inch or two back from its actual position.

Swing the clubhead up and down along the path you have visualized and try to hit the imaginary "ball."

This practice drill will automatically put more arm and hand action into your downswing. Thus you will also swing the golf club as you turn and clear your left hip to the left.

Should you begin to consistently take a divot behind the actual ball, merely focus on hitting the actual ball rather than the one that you have imagined.

Lesson 16

Diagnosis: You occasionally top your fairway shots along the ground and somewhat to the right of your target line. Sometimes you also catch turf behind the ball. You make your best shots when the ball is teed or sitting up well on fairway grass. Distance is not your worry, but you probably hit some of your chip shots and many of your sand shots "thin." In fact, the short game is where you suffer the most.

Explanation: Unlike the golfer who tops shots to the left because of an out-to-in clubhead path and a steeply downward angle of approach (*Lesson 15*), the shot pattern just described indicates an in-to-out path and an angle of approach that is too shallow. The clubhead reaches the bottom of its downward-upward arc before impact and is actually moving upward when it contacts the ball. Thus it has scraped the ground behind the ball and/or caught the top of the ball while moving upward. (*Illustration 8a* shows these impact conditions.)

Because the clubhead is moving upward by impact, these golfers make their best contact when the ball sits on a tee or high on fairway grass. They hit behind or top the ball that rests low in grass or sand.

Correction: Play the ball slightly farther forward in your stance—a bit more to the left. This will allow you to address the ball with your hips and shoulders aligned more to the left as, in your case, they should be.

This alignment will make you more conscious of your ball-target line. During the backswing, swing the club up along this line with your arms, making no effort to pivot. Clear your left hip to the left as you swing the club down to the ball with your arms.

These adjustments will make your clubhead path on line, rather than in to out, at impact. Thus its angle of approach will be level or slightly downward rather than upward. The bottom of your arc will occur at the ball rather than behind it.

Also, bear in mind that an in-to-out path is usually the result of a previous tendency to hook. Should that tendency reoccur, adjust your grip by turning both hands to the left at address (*see Illustration 18c*).

Lesson 17

Diagnosis: Your clubhead frequently takes turf from the ground behind the ball.

Explanation: As I explained in Lesson 9, the word "timing," to me, describes the relative movement of the golfer and his golf club, particularly during the downswing.

Ideally the golfer swings the club with his arms and hands as he moves and turns his legs and lower body to the left.

One's timing is poor when (a) the legs and body dominate or outrace the swinging of the club with the arms and hands, or when (b) the arms, hands and club outrace leg and hip movement.

Whereas the topping patterns described in Lessons 14 and 15 result from too much body action and not enough accompanying hand and arm effort, the tendency to hit fat shots is caused by insufficient leg and hip action. The arms and hands outrace the body and release the clubhead into the ground on the wrong side of the ball.

Correction: Position the ball and your hands farther forward to the left at address. This encourages an open body alignment—turned more to the left—which, in turn, helps the left hip clear to the left as the hands and arms continue to swing the club downward to the ball.

If you should start to top your shots, concentrate on swinging the club *down* from the top with your hands and arms. Conversely, heavy or fat shots will require you to concentrate on using more hip and leg action.

Lesson 18

Diagnosis: You frequently shank shots sharply to the right with the shorter iron clubs. The shots you do not shank usually finish left of target.

Explanation: The shanked shot is struck on the hosel (neck) of the club, rather than on the clubface. The club has moved outward during the downswing, farther away from the golfer than it had been originally positioned at address.

This outward movement on the downswing occurs because the overall swing is too flat. During the backswing the club has swung too far around and behind the player and insufficiently upward. Thus, during the downswing, it has moved too much around the player and forward—beyond the ball—instead of sufficiently downward.

The flat swing originates from the golfer's address position. He has seen or heard that good golfers hit their shorter iron shots from an open stance—as, indeed, they often do. (The left foot is set farther back than the right from the target line.)

Mistakes occur, however, when the shoulders are similarly aligned far around to the left, rather than parallel with the target line (*Illustration 26a*). This alignment also forces the ball to be too far forward in the stance, to the left of where it should be.

Since so much of this game is reaction, the address position I have described leads to far too much effort being made to get the club back to the inside so as to avoid hitting to the left where the player has aligned. This effort to get inside is bound to result in a backswing that is too flat (*Illustration 26a*). The club finishes the backswing while moving around and behind the player. Then it rebounds around and outward, beyond the ball, during the downswing. This creates the shank.

If the shot is not a shank, it is invariably a pull or a pull-hook to the left of target. The shot flies left because the ball is positioned too far left in the stance. By the time the clubhead finally reaches impact, it is already moving back to the inside, to the left, on the follow-through portion of its in-to-in arc. The clubface may also be closed to the left at impact, because the flat swing often makes it turn to the left too abruptly through the hitting area.

Correction: First bear in mind that the correct backswing is not only to the inside but upward as well.

Play the ball farther back to the right in your stance so that you can align your shoulders on target, rather than far to the left. This alignment to the inside will also eliminate the need for any conscious pivot to the right during your backswing in order to swing the club to the inside (*Illustration 26b*).

It will also allow you to visualize a path extending from the ball to the *inside* of your target line. Merely swing the club freely upward and downward with your arms and hands along the path that you have visualized.

An open stance is acceptable on shorter iron shots, but only if the shoulders are not similarly aligned to the left and the ball is not played too far forward. Aligning the shoulders too far left forces the backswing to be too flat—too far to the inside and insufficiently upward—if the shot is to be hit toward the target. If the backswing is too flat and *around* to the inside, the resulting downswing will also be too flat and *around* to the outside. This outward movement can cause shanking, since the club moves out beyond the ball and contact is made on its hosel. The open setup and forward ball positioning also cause pulling shots to the left when contact is made on the face of the club, since the arc is cutting to the inside again—to the left—by the time the club finally makes contact with the ball.

26b YES

Proper shoulder alignment and ball positioning allow you to swing the club somewhat to the inside on the backswing but sufficiently upward as well. When the backswing is sufficiently *upward* and somewhat to the inside, the normal reaction will be to swing sufficiently *downward* on the correct into-in path with the club moving, briefly, on line at impact.

Lesson 19

Diagnosis: Many shots are struck on the toe, or outer end, of the clubface.

Explanation: There are two distinctively different causes of hitting the ball off the toe of the club. The direction that your toed shots curve will tell you which explanation and correction apply in your particular case.

If your toed shots curve to the left, you will know that your clubface is closed—facing to the left of its path—at impact. When the face is turned to the left, the toe leads the heel into the ball so that contact is made on the former (*Illustration 27a*).

If your toed shots curve to the right, you will know that your swing is too upright (*Illustration 27b*). In that case your situation is the converse of the flat-swinging player who tends to shank shots off the opposite end of the clubface.

As I explained in Lesson 18, the flat-swinging golfer over-pivots during the backswing. Thus his club swings too far around behind him going back and, in reaction, too far outward in front of him going forward. The club moves out beyond the ball so that contact is made on its hosel.

Conversely, the upright swinger whose shots are hit on the toe does not swing the club *far enough* behind himself going back. Thus it does not move sufficiently outward in front of him going forward (*Illustration 27b*). Only the outer, toe portion of the clubface gets back to the target line and the ball.

Correction: If your toed shots curve to the left, you will need to adjust your grip to eliminate the early closing of the clubface. Set your hands on the club with each turned a bit farther to the left (*Illustration 27a*).

If your toed shots curve to the right, you will need to modify your posture at address so that you can swing on a less upright plane. Increase your knee flex slightly and decrease the amount that you bend your back and neck forward.

This posture will allow you to turn your right shoulder away to the inside—rather than to rock it upward—during your backswing. As you turn to the right, swing the club up and inside so that it finishes above the point of your right shoulder rather than over your head (*Illustration 27b*).

Toeing—2 Causes, 2 Cures

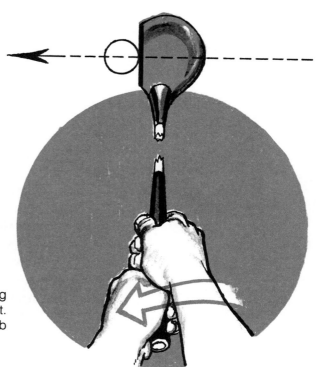

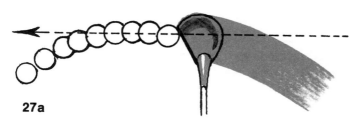

27a

Toed shots that curve left result from the clubface being closed at impact, so that the toe reaches the ball first. Eliminate the closed clubface by initially gripping the club with your hands turned a bit farther to the left.

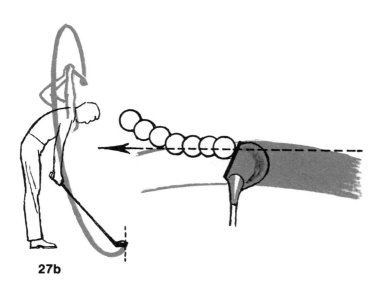

27b

Toed shots that curve to the right result from the swing being too upright. Since the club does not swing sufficiently behind the player and off the line during the backswing, it does not swing sufficiently outward in front of the player and back to the line during the downswing. Therefore, only the toe of the club returns to the ball. A more upright posture at address—more knee flex and less bending forward from the hips and neck—allows you to turn, rather than lift, your right shoulder during the backswing. This turning provides the inside element of the backswing that has been lacking.

Lesson 20

Diagnosis: Pitch shots fly on a straight line but to the left of target. Those that do not finish left usually come up short and often fly unusually high.

Explanation: When your short approach shots pull to the left, your clubhead is moving in that direction, on an out-to-in path, at impact. Your clubface is aligned more or less square to that path.

The shots that do not finish left usually come up short because, while your clubhead path is still to the left, your clubface is now aligned to the right of that path. The swing path to the left accompanied by the open face balance out to make the ball fly straight. It finishes short, however, because the open face has greatly increased the club's loft.

Actually, the shot I have just described is the exact type that old-time golfers were forced to play. The old gutta-percha balls that they used were rock-hard and, therefore, extremely difficult to fly on a suitably high trajectory for making them stop quickly, especially across the then-unwatered greens. These players needed a way to somehow increase loft and backspin on these shots.

The way they chose was to play this open-faced "cut" shot. By aiming the club to the right of target at address, they effectively increased its loft. By aligning their feet and shoulders to the left of target, they could easily swing to the left on an out-to-in path.

Swinging left with the face open not only makes the ball fly high and toward the target, but also tends to steepen the club's angle of approach, so that it puts more backspin on the ball.

Indeed, if these early golfers had played with our modern balls and on watered greens, they would not have needed to align so far to the left with the clubface so open when addressing their approach shots.

The cut shot that you now, sometimes, play inadvertently is, in truth, a nice shot to have in your golfing repertoire. Use it when you need an unusually high shot that will settle quickly on the green. (Do make sure, however, that you offset aligning your shoulders to the left and swinging in that direction by aiming the clubface to the right. Also plan for the shot to fly and roll a shorter distance than normal.)

In normal pitch-shot situations, however, this cut shot is less than ideal. It does not provide the distance and directional control that you need to make these shots finish on target consistently.

Please bear in mind that even on these shorter approach shots with the highly lofted irons, we still stand some distance to the side of the ball. Therefore the correct swing path is still from inside to straight to inside again. Our clubhead moves on target and faces on target for only a brief span in the hitting area. We should therefore address the ball in a way that will maximize our chances of actually making contact occur during that all-too-fleeting interval in our swings.

Correction: Standing to the short approach shot in a slightly open foot and hip position (*see Illustration 26b in Lesson 18*) will simplify clearing your left side to the left during your forward swing. This clearing to the left is desirable, largely because it improves your chances of swinging your arms through freely and, therefore, making contact with the clubface square to its path of movement.

However, for this path of movement to be along—not across—your target line, it is best if you address the ball with your shoulders aligned parallel to—not across—your target line (*see Illustration 26b*).

From the correct address position, you can swing the club to the ball from the inside as your left side clears to the left (*see Illustration 26b*). This gives your arms room to swing freely through to the target, allowing the hands to *release* the clubhead on line. This free release of the hands is most important in terms of hitting these short shots the correct distance.

Lesson 21

Diagnosis: Inconsistent contact—"fat" or "thin"—is made on short approach shots.

Explanation: Of the four impact factors, the most important on these short shots from around the green is the clubhead's angle of approach to the ball.

On these relatively simple strokes, most weekend golfers can swing the club on more or less the right path and align the clubface more or less square to that path. (And even an open clubface is not likely to spin the ball sideways an appreciable amount on these short shots.)

Now, most mishit shots occur because the clubhead reaches the bottom of its arc before it gets back to the ball. It may touch down and snag in the grass behind the ball—the "fat" shot (*Illustration 28b*)—or it may skim the middle or top of the ball while moving upward—the "thin" shot (*Illustration 28c*). In either case it is the club's level or upward, rather than downward, angle of approach that causes the poor contact.

While the obvious solution is simply to swing the clubhead somewhat downward to the ball, this is difficult for many golfers to do consistently until they first eliminate any need, conscious or subconscious, to "help" the ball into the air by swinging the club upward to it.

Correction: Always visualize the shot you want to play *before* you choose a club. Consider the lie of the ball in the grass, and the distance and terrain between it and the flagstick. Decide where you want the ball to land. "See" the trajectory that would fly the ball to that spot and, thereafter, cause it to bounce and roll to the hole.

After thus visualizing the shot, decide which club would most likely create it. Do not choose that club, however. Instead, select a club with *more* loft than you think you need, one that you think will fly the ball *higher* than you want the shot to fly.

In short, eliminate beforehand any need to help the ball into the air.

Finally, set up to the shot so that you can contact the ball with a downward moving clubhead. Play the ball far enough *back* in your stance (to the right) with your hands far enough *forward* of it (to the left) so that you must catch the ball during your downswing, before the clubhead reaches the bottom of its arc (*Illustration 28a*).

The ball will fly into the air, even with the clubhead moving

28a

LAG A°

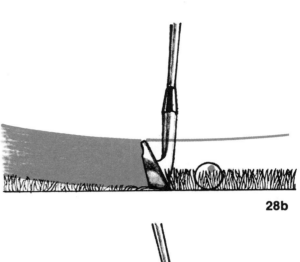

28b

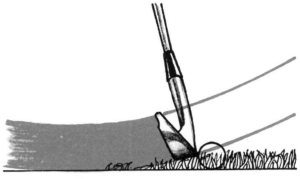

28c

downward, because you have chosen a club with more loft than you really need.

A simple but effective drill to develop the downward angle of approach on these shots is also shown in *Illustration 28a*. Note that a second ball is placed about 10–12 inches behind the original. Try to hit the original without your clubhead touching the rearward ball, during either your backswing or downswing. You will find that any attempt to lift or scoop the original ball into the air will cause your club to hit the rearward ball instead.

Lesson 22

Diagnosis: Occasional spells of poor contact on less-than-full approach shots and putts. These shots usually finish well short of the hole.

Explanation: Length of backswing, while not a particularly significant measure of good golf on the full shots, is an important factor on these shorter shots.

On full shots we tend to make about as much backswing as we sense we can comfortably control. This seldom requires much conscious attention. We simply swing our normal length.

On less than full shots, however, we need backswings of more specific lengths. The length should be such that, with normal acceleration thereafter, the ball will go the correct distance.

A backswing that is too long will, of course, send the ball too far if the contact is solid. More often, however, a too-long backswing breeds a decelerating forward swing that misconnects with the ball.

A backswing that is too short—the more common situation—invariably causes a quick overuse of the body during the forward swing. We tend to apply ourselves to the shot to make up for the lack of backswing that we sense. Solid contact is all too rare.

Correction: First you must discover if your backswing on these shots tends to be too long or too short. If it is too long you will, upon reflection, be extremely aware of having made a backswing. If your backswing is too short, you will have absolutely no recollection of your swing from the time you started the club away from the ball. I promise that this is true.

Another way to detect if your backswing tends to be too long or too short is to reflect upon the shape of your full shots. If your long shots usually curve to the left, it is quite probable that you misconnect on short shots because your backswing is too long. If your long shots usually curve to the right, beware of too little backswing on your short shots.

Once you pinpoint whether or not your backswing is too long or too short—don't be afraid to experiment—merely hit some practice shots, including putts, with backswings of corrective lengths. Your contact should improve straightaway.

Also, on these shots I suggest that you form the habit of making several, smoothly accelerating practice swings beforehand. Try to find and sense the length of swing that will make the ball go the distance in question with the club you have in hand. You will not find, and then duplicate, the perfect length every time. You will, however, strike more solid shots closer to the hole than you had before.

Lesson 23

Diagnosis: Generally poor putting. Seldom do your long putts approximate the right distance. No confidence on the shorter putts.

Explanation: Regarding putting, the first suggestion I make to pupils is that they not change their style if they already putt well. Good putting depends so much on using your own natural gifts. It would be foolish to change something that is natural and successful for you simply because it does not conform to John Jacobs', or anyone else's, putting ideals.

However, if your putting fits the above diagnosis, it almost follows that your technique will be at fault. To show you what I mean, I would ask that you stand and face a wall. Position yourself about arms' length from it.

Extend your arms toward the wall and start clapping your hands as you do when applauding. As you clap, gradually widen the sweep of your arms.

I'm sure that this will all feel natural. Even a small child can clap his hands soundly together.

You will also notice that, as you swing your hands farther and farther apart, they also move farther and farther away from the wall. This, too, is *natural*. And this movement away from the straight wall should similarly happen whenever we swing from alongside a target line, as we do on golf shots.

Because we stand relatively close to the ball when putting, the distance that our arms, hands and putterhead should swing to the inside of our target line is very slight, even on very long putts. It is, however, natural—and therefore vital—that the putter does swing somewhat to the inside on all except the very short putts.

To prove this to yourself, merely clap alongside the wall once again. This time, however, make sure that your hands do not move away from the wall as they swing apart. You will immediately feel inhibited. You will feel muscular tension. You will find it somewhat more difficult to make your hands clap soundly together.

Swinging the putter on line throughout your putting stroke similarly takes away from your natural gifts. One of these natural gifts is to square the putterface to your putting line by the time contact occurs, just as you squared your palms to each other when clapping. Another natural gift is to swing the putterhead into the ball on a relatively level angle of approach, so that the ball will roll smoothly forward without first hopping or skid-

Putt Like You Clap

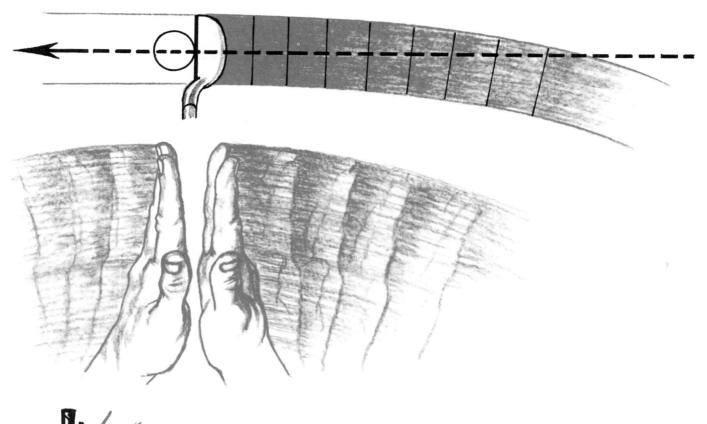

29

Putting should be as natural as clapping. Hold the putter with your palms facing and aligned with the putterface. Align yourself parallel with your intended putting line. Swing the putterhead from inside to along your line as shown. The amount of inside movement on the backstroke will depend on the length of your stroke. Thereafter the putter should gradually return to the line and continue on line well past the ball's position. This path keeps the putterhead moving close to the ground for better rolling of the ball, whereas the purely on-line stroke forces it to raise and lower during the backstroke and downstroke. The proper path also allows for a natural squaring of the face to the line at contact, just as the right hand claps squarely against the left. The natural stroke allows your instincts to roll the putt the correct distance.

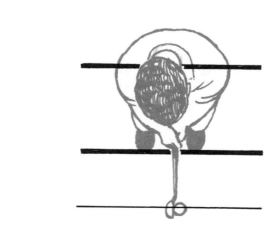

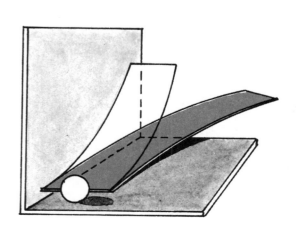

ding. Another natural instinct is to freely release the clubhead into the ball at the right speed to make the putt go the correct distance.

All of these natural and correct instincts tend to lessen whenever we contrive a putting stroke that is unnatural. As clapping alongside the wall has shown, the putting stroke that is on line throughout is, indeed, unnatural.

Correction: First hold the putter with your palms facing each other and aligned with the putterface, just as they would be if you had clapped them together (*Illustration 29*). Also, stand "square," aligned parallel to the line on which you intend the putt to start.

Next practise making strokes in which the putterhead gradually moves inside the line during the backstroke, retraces that path back to the ball and, thereafter, continues forward along the line (*Illustration 29*). (On long putts the putterhead will, eventually, return inside on the follow-through.)

I suggest that you practise these strokes alongside the base of a wall. There it will be apparent when your putterhead fails to swing to and from the inside. Outdoors you can do this same drill alongside the shaft of another club that you have laid on the ground. You will eventually find how much you need to be inside on the backstroke in order to swing on line through the ball position.

As you make these strokes, learn to feel the difference between a natural and correct stroke from inside to along the line and the unnatural on-line or across-the-line strokes. Accept the fact that the natural stroke, though correct, may feel unnatural to you for a time if your previous stroke was unnatural.

Finally, I would add that the face of the club should remain square to the clubhead path—not the target line—throughout the stroke. This, too, will happen naturally, as in clapping, with a little practice.

Lesson 24

Diagnosis: Inconsistent bunker shots. Some stay in the sand, many fly over the green.

Explanation: Straightaway I should warn you against trying to pick the ball clean from sand around the green, as many weekend golfers attempt to do. This approach presents a problem that even expert golfers avoid. The problem is simply that these are short shots. Thus they require a minimal amount of clubhead speed if the contact is to be clean. If any sand is taken, as usually happens, the club is not moving fast enough for the ball to carry forth from the bunker.

The wise golfer avoids this whole situation by making a fairly long and authoritative swing, even on extremely short bunker shots. His shots do not fly too far, however, because the clubhead never actually contacts the ball. Instead it swings into the sand well behind the ball. It displaces a cushion of sand which, in turn, displaces the ball. The ball flies free of the bunker while riding on this cushion. It does not fly too far because this same cushion, interfering as it does between the clubhead and the ball, also deadens the force of the blow.

While swinging the clubhead into the sand behind and under the ball's position is the preferred technique, it does require a steeply downward angle of approach. If the approach is too shallow, it may not displace enough sand to cushion the blow; the ball will fly and roll too far. Or the shallow approach can cause the clubhead to skim into the sand too far behind the ball and then rebound upward into the top of it. The topped shot rolls only a few feet forward.

You may recall that in the section on impact factors, I explained the relationship between clubhead path and angle of approach. There (*see Illustration 8a*) you will see that the more the swing path back to the ball is from the inside of the target line, the shallower the angle of approach tends to be. The more the path is from out to in (*see Illustration 8b*), the steeper the angle of approach becomes.

Thus, since the steep angle of approach is best for penetrating sand behind the ball, the out-to-in clubhead path is best on most bunker shots. A normal swing path, such as might be ideal on drives and most fairway shots, creates an angle of approach that is simply too shallow for the normal sand shot.

If your sand shots vary from being too short to too long, especially if they tend toward being too long, it is quite possible

Playing the Basic Sand Shot

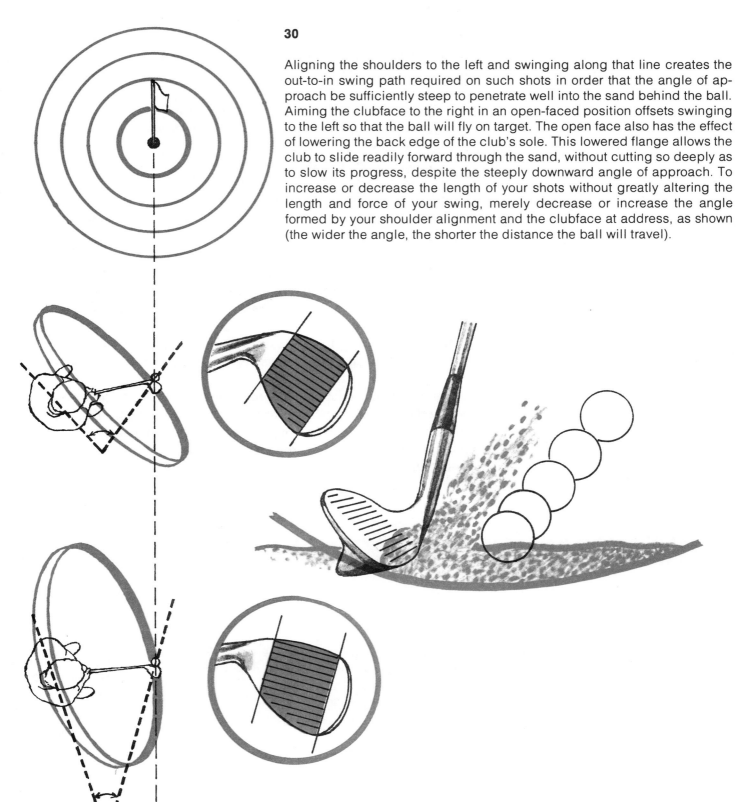

30

Aligning the shoulders to the left and swinging along that line creates the out-to-in swing path required on such shots in order that the angle of approach be sufficiently steep to penetrate well into the sand behind the ball. Aiming the clubface to the right in an open-faced position offsets swinging to the left so that the ball will fly on target. The open face also has the effect of lowering the back edge of the club's sole. This lowered flange allows the club to slide readily forward through the sand, without cutting so deeply as to slow its progress, despite the steeply downward angle of approach. To increase or decrease the length of your shots without greatly altering the length and force of your swing, merely decrease or increase the angle formed by your shoulder alignment and the clubface at address, as shown (the wider the angle, the shorter the distance the ball will travel).

that your clubhead path is too much from the inside, thus making your angle of approach too shallow.

Correction: Address the ball in sand as you would for playing a fairway wedge shot, but align your shoulders farther to the left of target (*Illustration 30*). Also, aim the clubface to the right of target, as shown.

Aligning to the left will help you swing in that direction, as you should do. This out-to-in clubhead path will help provide the steeper angle of approach.

Aiming with the clubface open offsets swinging to the left; the shot flies on target. Also, the open clubface allows the lower back flange of your sand iron to readily glide forward through the sand, much like a rudder, without cutting too far in despite the initially steep penetration (*Illustration 30*).

You will also notice in *Illustration 30* that there is an angle formed between the lines that indicate shoulder alignment to the left and clubface aim to the right. As a general rule you will find that the larger you make this angle at address—the farther you align left and aim right—the shorter distance the ball will travel with a given force of swing. Thus by increasing this angle you can actually swing quite aggressively, even on very short greenside shots.

Summing up: Clubface open, shoulders open at address. Swing the club up and down along the original shoulder line with the hands and arms. Clear the left hip to the left while swinging through to allow room for the arms to swing on the desired out-to-in path.

Lesson 25

Diagnosis: Bunker shots from around the green often finish short of target. Clubhead cuts too far into the sand.

Explanation: If cutting too far into the sand is your problem, I would first ask if you do, in fact, use a sand wedge on these shots. If not, the club that you do use is probably a large part of the fault.

In *Illustration 31* you will see that the bottom edge of the sand wedge angles upward slightly from back to front. The bottom edge of the pitching wedge angles downward, as do the soles of all other fairway irons.

It is the upward angling of the sand wedge sole that keeps this club from penetrating too far downward into the sand when it is used correctly. Because it can displace a relatively shallow cut of sand, it loses relatively little clubhead speed in the process. Enough remains to readily displace both sand and ball.

The downward angling of the fairway iron, however, makes it cut too deep into all sand except that which is exceptionally hard-packed or wet. The deep cut leaves too much sand between club and ball, and too little clubhead speed to readily displace either.

Thus the sand wedge can be a valuable tool, especially if you often must play from bunkers that are filled with soft sand.

If you already use a sand wedge but still cut too far under the ball, it will be a closed clubface that is largely responsible. As you can see in *Illustration 31* even the raised leading edge of the sand wedge becomes turned downward when the clubface is closed to the left. In effect, the sand wedge then becomes a pitching wedge.

Correction: You may be able to avoid the closed clubface and its penetrative effect if you merely aim the clubface to the right of target while aligning your shoulders—and then swinging—well to the left, as I suggested in Lesson 24.

If you should continue to cut too far under the ball, however, you will also need to stress clearing your left hip to the left while swinging through. This will bring your clubhead through the sand trailing your hands and with the clubface still open (*Illustration 31*). This open clubface will keep the sole angled upward. Thus, after initially penetrating the sand, it will gradually level out and glide forward instead of continuing downward.

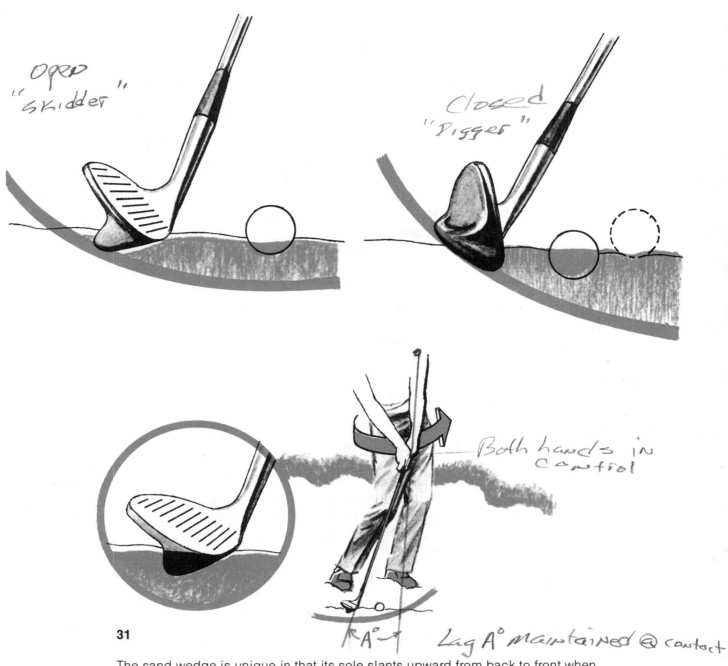

Open
"Skidder"

Closed
"Digger"

Both hands in control

31

Lag A° maintained @ contact

The sand wedge is unique in that its sole slants upward from back to front when the face is squarely aligned (*upper left illustration*). The lower back edge acts as a skid so that the clubhead does not penetrate too far under the ball despite its initial downward movement into the sand. This skid effect is lost, however, when the clubface is closed (*upper right illustration*). Then the leading edge turns downward, creating deeper penetration. While the deeper cut is ideal when the ball is buried, it is too deep for the ball that is not. Then too much sand intervenes between the club and the ball. The shot usually finishes short of target. To avoid closing the face, concentrate on clearing the left hip to the left on the throughswing so that your hands lead the clubhead through the sand (*bottom illustration*). This holds the clubface slightly open so that the skid effect can take place.

SUGGESTIONS FOR ON-COURSE SITUATIONS

THE FIRST PART of this book has been about improving your shots. The sections that follow will deal with ways to improve your scores.

Obviously better shotmaking will help you shoot lower scores, especially if you recognize your own personal skills and limitations. As a general rule, you will score better if you attempt only those shots you know you can play fairly well and do not attempt the others.

These decisions I must leave to you. Unfortunately, I cannot be on hand to assess your ability and to advise you accordingly as you play the course. What I can and will do, however, is open your mind to certain on-course possibilities and limitations that are universal to *all* players.

In the final analysis, golf is a game of ball control, a matter of creating the impact conditions that will cause the ball to do what you want it to do. There are, however, certain playing situations that make this easier than you might have realized. You should be made aware of these possibilities. You should use them to your advantage.

Conversely, there are certain on-course situations that make it very difficult for even the great golfers to create the impact conditions—and thus the shot—they would like.

These players have reached the stage where their experience and knowledge make them aware of what is possible. However, the weekend golfer, lacking this knowledge and experience, makes decisions that cause his scores to be much higher than his ability would warrant.

In short, Dear Reader, you probably need certain ballistic information that will allow you to play the right shot at the right time and to avoid the wrong shot at the wrong time.

For instance, I was well into my playing career before I understood why so many of my wedge shots finished well left of my target. I had been trying to curve these shots into the flagstick from the left because I knew that the left-to-right shot should settle quickly on the green. Only at that advanced stage in my golfing life, however, did I finally realize that because this extremely lofted club strikes the underside of the ball it applies considerable backspin but very little, if any, slice spin. Curving wedge shots to the right is almost impossible.

On the other hand, it is relatively easy to fade a drive to the right. Its relatively straight face contacts the diameter of the ball so that sidespin is readily applied.

Earlier in my career I found another shot that is ballistically difficult and therefore risky even for most good golfers. This is the drive that is meant to curve just slightly to the left, perhaps away from an out-of-bounds on the right. I realized that to make the ball curve slightly left the clubface must be closed slightly to the left at impact. However, since closing the face decreases the club's effective loft, and since the driver carries only limited loft to begin with, this is obviously very dangerous. It does not need much closing of the face to create minus loft. The club can actually face downward, as well as left, at impact. The shot does not get off the ground.

These are examples of things I will explain in the upcoming pages. I suspect that many of my explanations and suggestions will cover aspects of playing golf that have never occurred to you before. Hopefully this information will help you make better decisions on the course and thus improve your scores straight-away, apart from working on your shots along lines that I have suggested in the earlier lessons.

Situation 1

Suggestions: Unless you consistently curve your shots slightly to the left with the driver, this is a good time to consider leaving it in the bag. Two ballistic factors favour using a 3-wood or 4-wood instead in this situation.

First, these clubs are more lofted and shallower-faced than the driver. Thus they usually make contact lower on the back of the ball. The lower contact adds backspin and lessens sidespin. This reduces the degree that the ball will slice into the trouble on the right if you should happen to hit it with an open clubface (*Illustration 32a*).

Second, bear in mind that if you should happen to make contact with the clubface closed to the left, the club will be carrying a reduced degree of effective loft. Thus the more-lofted 3-wood or 4-wood would be more likely to fly the ball a suitable height than would the straighter-faced driver, which might fail to put the ball into the air at all (*Illustration 32b*).

The golfer who slices almost all long shots should surely choose a more-lofted club in this situation. He would also be wise to grip the club with his hands turned a little more to the right (*see Lesson 1*). This will make it easier for him to square the clubface at impact.

For many golfers it also helps to tee the ball a bit higher than normal in this situation. The higher the ball sits, the more we tend to sweep it away with a somewhat flatter swing. This, in itself, generally squares the clubface a bit sooner in the hitting area.

32a

All things being equal, the lesser loft of the driver (*left-hand illustration*) creates initial contact that is higher on the ball than that made with a more-lofted club (*right-hand illustration*). Since the higher contact creates more sidespin and less backspin, driver shots made with an open clubface will curve farther to the right than will shots that are similarly struck with a more-lofted club.

32b

The extra loft of a 3-wood or 4-wood (*right-hand illustration*) is also advantageous if impact should occur with the clubface closed. Since closing a clubface reduces loft, the less-lofted driver (*left-hand illustration*) might not carry enough effective loft to make the ball go into the air.

Situation 2

Situation: Driving on a hole that has trouble on the left.

Suggestions: This situation should not be particularly bothersome for the golfer who invariably slices his drives to the right. With trouble on the left, this is his safest shot.

To further guarantee the slice, however, he might well choose a driver rather than a more-lofted club, if he happens to be in doubt about club selection. As I explained in Situation 1 (*see Illustration 32a*), because the driver has less loft and a deeper face it tends to contact the ball higher on its backside. This higher contact decreases backspin. Thus any slice spin applied will make the ball curve to the right a greater degree.

The golfer who tends to curve his drives to the left will find it helps to tee the ball a bit lower than normal in this situation. With the ball sitting lower to the ground, he will be less likely to sweep it away with a relatively flat swing, which tends to close the clubface to the left prematurely in the hitting area. Instead he will instinctively swing on a slightly more upright plane, which tends to delay the squaring of the clubface.

This golfer will also find that a tighter right-hand grip will, as I explained in Lesson 7, further reduce any hooking tendency, which in this situation could prove disastrous.

Situation 3

Situation: Playing in a left-to-right crosswind.

Suggestions: Most right-handed golfers hit their worst shots when the wind is blowing from left to right. They sense that they must start the shot out to the left to offset the wind. This causes them to swing the club back to the ball from *outside* the target line while— bearing in mind that we stand to the side of the ball—the ideal path is from the *inside*.

Also, as I explained earlier (*see Illustration 8b*) the out-to-in path creates a steeply downward angle of approach. This not only reduces distance, because the blow is downward rather than forward, but it also inhibits free swinging of the arms and hands, for fear of burying the clubhead into the ground. This lack of free swinging impedes squaring of the clubface; at impact it still faces to the right, in the direction that the wind is blowing.

Thus it is best to avoid the instinctive temptation to swing the club to the left of where you are aiming—out to in—when playing in a left-to-right wind. There are better ways to handle this type of wind. The method you choose, however, should depend on the shot you happen to be playing.

For instance, on a tee shot where you want maximum distance, I suggest, given a wide fairway, you merely play a straight shot down the left side, with the club swinging back to the ball from the *inside,* and allow the wind to curve it back to the centre of the fairway. Since the ball will be curving in somewhat the same direction as the wind is blowing, this method will give you good distance.

If, however, the fairway is too narrow to allow the ball to drift to the right with the wind, you will need to play a shot that would normally curve slightly to the left. The wind will offset this normal curve and hold the shot more or less on a straight line.

To play this shot you will need to hit the ball with the clubface turned slightly to the left of your swing path. Since closing the clubface takes loft off the club (*see Illustration 32b*), I suggest you choose a 3-wood rather than a driver for this shot. The relatively straight-faced driver, when closed, does not carry enough loft to give the shot sufficient height. However, the 3-wood when closed becomes, in effect, a 2-wood or a driver. It will give your shot a trajectory that is more or less normal.

To hit the shot with a slightly closed clubface, grip the 3-wood with your hands turned a bit farther to the right than normal, as

I suggest in Lesson 1. Aim and swing for a straight shot, ignoring the wind.

When hitting approach shots to the green in a left-to-right wind, you again have the same two options. You can either aim to the left and let the wind bring the ball into the flagstick, or you can aim on target and hit a shot that would normally curve to the left, one that will fight the wind and thus stop quickly.

On long approach shots with, say, a 2-, 3- or 4-iron, the first option is best. Any attempt to hit these relatively straight-faced irons with a closed clubface would probably leave you with too little effective loft to give the shot sufficient height. Therefore, aim left of target, play a straight shot and let the wind bring it in. The ball will probably bound freely forward and to the right upon landing, however, so plan to land it short of the green and somewhat to the left.

On occasion you may also use this method on shorter approach shots with the more-lofted irons. These shots will fly higher, of course, so you can try to land the ball on the green, left and short of the flagstick, but only if the green is very soft and the flagstick is near the back. Otherwise this plan of action would be dangerous. The ball will be curving from the left, thus flying more or less with the wind. It may not hold the putting surface.

Therefore, as a general rule I suggest that you apply your second option when approaching with a more-lofted iron club in the left-to-right wind. Play the shot that would normally curve left but, because of the counteracting wind, will tend to hold its line. This shot will settle softly on most greens.

To play this shot I suggest you choose a club with more loft than you would normally use for the distance at hand, say an 8-iron instead of a 7-iron, or a 7-iron instead of a 6-iron. With less club in hand, you will need to swing full-out, giving the shot an especially forceful lash with your arms and hands. This extra effort will tend to close the clubface slightly at impact so that the ball can fight the wind and thus hold its line.

You would not want to use this method if you have found that swinging with extra arm and hand action makes you mishit your shots. In that case I suggest you choose the club that you would normally use for the approach shot in question, but make the same grip adjustment that I just suggested for tee shots when fighting the left-to-right wind with a 3-wood.

Situation 4

Situation: Playing in a right-to-left crosswind.

Suggestions: The right-handed golfer who normally makes the mistake of swinging on an out-to-in clubhead path will hit some of his best shots when the wind is blowing from right to left. He senses that he needs to start the ball to the right to offset the wind. Thus he swings the club into the ball from the inside as opposed to his normal out-to-in approach.

As I have explained, when the clubhead's path is from the inside rather than the outside, its angle of approach is shallower (*see Illustration 8a*). This sends the force of the blow forward, rather than downward, so the shot travels farther. The path from the inside also encourages a free release of the arms and hands into the shot. This tends to square the clubface on target at impact, rather than leave it open to the right.

When driving down an open fairway in a right-to-left wind, I suggest you merely play a normal drive down the right side of the fairway. Let the wind bring it into the centre of the fairway. The ball will travel good distance because it will be curving in somewhat the same direction as the wind is blowing.

If the fairway is too narrow to allow the ball to drift to the left, you will need to play a drive that would normally curve to the right. The right-to-left wind will disallow much of this curve and thus hold the ball more or less on line. This shot should be simple for golfers whose drives normally curve to the right. Others should grip the club with their hands turned a little farther to the left than normal, as I explained in Lesson 7. This grip will delay the squaring of the clubface so that it still faces slightly to the right at impact, to counteract the right-to-left wind.

Teeing the ball lower than normal has this same counteracting effect. With the ball setting close to the ground we tend to swing more steeply downward to it, to avoid the ground behind it. The steeper angle of approach, in turn, tends to leave the clubface slightly open at impact.

When approaching to the green in a right-to-left wind, it is also best to hit a shot that would normally curve to the right. Again, the wind will hold the ball on line. Since the ball is more or less fighting the wind, it will settle quickly upon landing, whereas the shot that is allowed to drift to the left, with the wind, will not.

On these approach shots I suggest you choose more club than you would normally use for the distance in question—a 7-iron rather than an 8-iron, or a 6-iron instead of a 7-iron. Knowing that you have too much club in hand, you will instinctively swing with less force than normal. The less-forceful swing will tend to leave the clubface slightly open to the right at impact. This puts a certain amount of left-to-right spin on the ball to offset the right-to-left wind.

Please bear in mind, however, that it is most difficult to apply slice spin to the ball with the more-lofted irons, such as the wedges and 9-iron. These lofted clubs contact the ball so low on its underside that in large part backspin, rather than slice spin, is applied.

Situation 5

You face a shot from a "tight" lie. The ball rests either atop bare ground or well down in the grass.

Suggestions: In either of these tight-lie situations, your clubhead must first contact the low-lying ball, not the barren ground or too much of any grass that might be behind it.

To catch the ball first the most important impact condition to create is a fairly steep angle of approach. The clubhead that reaches the ball while still moving downward will have already passed over the bare ground or much of the grass, whichever the problem may be (*Illustration 33a*).

There are two excellent ways to steepen your club's angle of approach. However, each tends to create an entirely different type of ball flight. One makes shots fly a relatively short distance on a rather high trajectory. The ball settles quickly upon landing. The other method produces low-flying, running shots that travel farther overall.

I suggest that in any tight-lie situation you first decide which of these two types of shots you would prefer. Then apply the downswing-steepening technique that is more likely to create that shot.

The method of steepening your angle of approach that results in the high, short shot (*Illustration 33b*) involves swinging the club through impact on an out-to-in path. First align your shoulders farther to the left than you normally would. Then swing the clubhead parallel to that leftward alignment through impact.

To make this shot fly on target, rather than to the left in the direction you are swinging, open the clubface a bit to the right of target at address. Set your hands a little forward, to the left of the clubhead, as well. Maintain the open face through impact by making sure that your hands lead the clubhead into the hitting area. Because of the open face, you should allow for the shot to curve to the right except when using a highly lofted club. The amount of curve to plan for will increase with the length of the shot.

These shots usually fly higher than normal and settle quickly upon landing because the open clubface increases loft. The added loft will make the shot fly a shorter distance, however, as will the glancing blow that comes from swinging to the left with the clubface opened to the right. Thus a 6-iron, for instance, might easily produce an "8-iron" shot.

Actually, this particular technique for steepening the angle of approach is almost the same as I recommended—for the same

2 Ways to Play from Tight Lies

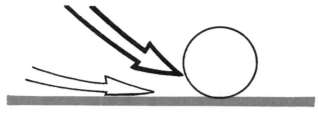

33a

Tight lies require a steep angle of approach so that the clubhead passes over the bare ground or much of the grass behind the ball, whichever the case may be. There are two ways to steepen your angle of approach. You can either swing on an out-to-in path with the clubface open, which results in a shorter and higher shot with relatively little roll (*see Illustration 33b*), or you can contact the ball earlier in your downswing, well before the clubhead reaches the bottom of its arc, which results in a longer, lower, forward-running shot (*33c*). Your choice of swing-steepening technique should depend on the type of shot result you wish to achieve.

33b

To play the higher, shorter, quick-stopping shot, align your shoulders farther left than normal and aim your clubface farther right. Set your hands slightly ahead of the clubhead and retain this relationship through impact. Swing the club up and down with your arms so that it moves parallel to your original shoulder alignment—thus on an out-to-in path—through impact.

33c

To play the lower, longer forward-running shot, play the ball well back in your stance with your hands set well forward, thus hooding the clubface. This will set most of your weight on your left foot. Swing the clubhead up and down along your target line, predominantly with your arms.

reason—on normal sand shots from greenside bunkers (*Lesson 24*). It differs only in that the club swings downward to the ball rather than into sand behind it.

The second way to steepen your angle in tight-lie situations (*shown in Illustration 33c*) is, in fact, identical to the method I suggest for sand shots from fairway bunkers. In each case you should play the ball farther back to the right in your stance than normal. In each case you would set your hands well forward, to the left of the clubhead, in more or less their normal position relative to your left thigh.

This combination of ball back and hands forward, if maintained through impact, assures that contact will occur before the clubhead has completed the downswing portion of its arc. To further assure a descending angle of approach, address the ball with more weight on your left side and with your right shoulder slightly higher than normal. Swing the club up and down the target line on a fairly upright plane predominantly with your arms.

This shot will usually fly lower and run farther than normal because the ball-back, hands-forward combination "hoods" (delofts) the clubface. That same 6-iron that I said might create "8-iron" shots with the first tight-lie solution mentioned might well produce "4-iron" shots if you apply this second approach to the problem.

Situation 6

Situation: Your ball is in the rough, say 4-iron distance from the green. You would like to use that club so as to reach your target. However, you have found in the past that you do not contact the ball solidly on shots from rough with the longer, less-lofted clubs.

Suggestions: This is another situation where the weekend golfer often wastes strokes. He bows to the temptation to go for the green with the club that he would normally use from the fairway at that distance. As it swings into the ball, however, the clubhead snags in the intervening grass. All too often the ball finishes far short of the desired distance.

I suggest that in this sort of situation you first choose a club with more loft than you would normally use, in this case say a 7-iron instead of the 4-iron.

Play the ball farther back in your stance than normal (*see Illustration 33c*). (The deeper the lie, the farther back you should play the ball and the more-lofted club you should choose.) Do not, however, set your hands any farther to the right than their normal position at address.

With your hands well forward of the clubhead, you will find it easy to swing the club more abruptly upward and downward than normal. The steeper angle of approach into the ball avoids most of the grass behind it and thus makes the impact more direct.

The better contact makes the shot go farther. So too does the fact that the 7-iron's steep approach has, in effect, reduced its loft, perhaps even to that of the 4-iron you would have preferred to use in the first place.

Usually the shot will fly lower than you would normally expect from the club in hand. It will generally roll much farther, however, perhaps as far as the green. Therefore you should take into account beforehand the problems posed by any intervening hazards.

Situation 7

Situation: Some object—perhaps a tree or bush—blocks your line to the target. It seems impossible to play over or under the object. The choice is either a straight shot safely away from the problem or a curved shot around it.

Suggestions: I find that this situation causes many golfers to attempt shots that cannot possibly succeed. The shot that they intend should curve flies straight or the intended straight shot curves.

The golfer blames his poor swing on bad luck. He resolves to get it right next time. But he will fail again and again, until he finally realizes that talent alone will not succeed on some shots in golf. There are certain conditions that make certain shots all but unplayable, even for a Jack Nicklaus.

Conditions affect what your club can do or cannot do to the golf ball: *the ballistics of impact.* I want to make you aware of these conditions so that you will not attempt to avoid the object in question with a risky or impossible shot but, instead, will play the shot that conditions more or less favour.

The conditions you should consider in this sort of situation, apart from any crosswind or any slicing or hooking tendency you might have, are (a) the length of the shot, (b) the lie of the ball and (c) any sloping terrain in the immediate area.

Length of shot. All things being equal, it is possible to curve long shots in either direction. Since these shots call for a minimum of clubface loft, the contact will be high enough on the back of the ball to apply sidespin.

In most instances, however, impact ballistics favour playing the longer shots from left to right, not right to left.

This is true because the right-to-left shot calls for an in-to-out swing path with the clubface closed to the left of that path at impact. Since the closed face delofts the club, the straighter-faced woods and longer iron clubs may not carry enough effective loft at impact to put the ball into the air. Therefore you must be sure to choose a club with more loft than you would normally select. A 5-iron, for instance, might actually translate into a 2-iron or 3-iron at impact.

Moreover, the long right-to-left shot requires an exceptionally good lie, since the in-to-out path makes the angle of approach very shallow, especially with the longer-shafted clubs. The ball must be sitting up perfectly so that the shallow-moving clubhead can contact it solidly without catching in grass or turf behind it.

Conversely, long shots can be played from left to right with far less risk. This shape requires an out-to-in path with the

How Conditions Affect the Curve of Shots (apart from crosswinds)

Conditions that favour playing a left-to-right shot, but make the right-to-left shot risky, if not impossible, are the following:

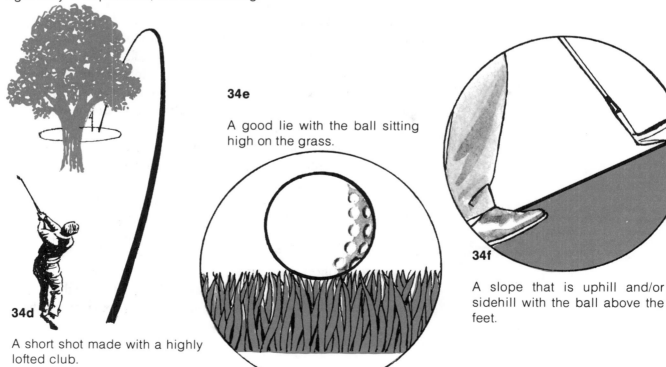

34a

A long shot that requires the use of a relatively straight-faced club.

34b

A lie that is tight.

34c

A slope that is downhill and/or sidehill with the ball resting below the feet.

Conditions that favour playing a right-to-left shot, but make slicing from left to right risky or impossible, are the following:

34d

A short shot made with a highly lofted club.

34e

A good lie with the ball sitting high on the grass.

34f

A slope that is uphill and/or sidehill with the ball above the feet.

clubface open. The out-to-in path creates a relatively steep angle of approach so that the contact can be fairly solid even if lie is less than ideal. Also, since the open clubface increases loft, it becomes relatively easy to get the ball well into the air with the straighter-faced clubs. The added loft will, however, reduce the length that you can expect from the club in hand.

Short shots played around an object are all but impossible to curve from left to right. The extra loft that results from the required open clubface, when added to the already highly lofted irons, makes contact occur well to the underside of the ball. This low contact puts so much backspin on the ball that it cannot be curved to the right.

It can be curved from right to left, however, thus making this the preferable shape on short shots. With the highly lofted clubs enough loft remains, despite the required closed face, to easily get the shot into the air. Moreover, with the loft decreased by the closed face, contact occurs high enough on the ball to apply the right-to-left sidespin needed to make the ball curve.

The lie of the ball. A good lie with plenty of grass under the ball simplifies playing a right-to-left shot but makes slicing more difficult. Conversely, as I have said, the tight lie on barren ground makes slicing relatively easy but renders the right-to-left shots practically unplayable.

When the ball sits high on the grass, the human instinct is to sweep it away with a relatively flat swing. This type of swing encourages the clubface to close rapidly in the hitting area, thus facilitating the right-to-left shape. Moreover, with the ball ideally situated on the grass, solid contact is possible despite the relatively shallow angle of approach that results from the in-to-out clubhead path.

When we have the opposite sort of lie, with the ball resting on barren ground, both human instinct and golf ballistics favour slicing.

First, we sense that it would be difficult to contact such a low-lying ball solidly if we made a flat, sweeping swing. Instead we tend to attack it with a somewhat steep angle of approach. This, in itself, tends to leave the clubface open at impact, just as it should be for curving shots to the right.

Second, as I have said, the open clubface needed for slicing also has the effect of increasing the club's loft. This extra loft sends the ball well into the air despite the tightness of the lie.

The tight lie, however, all but disallows the right-to-left shot, other than with the highly lofted irons. This shape calls for a closed clubface and a shallow in-to-out swing path. With the ball resting tight to the ground, the straighter-faced club cannot make solid contact with the bottom of the ball. However, since the shorter irons force us to stand closer to the ball and, therefore, swing on a more upright plane, it is possible to make solid contact with these clubs even when the lie is tight.

The immediate terrain. As a general rule, you will find it relatively easy to slice, and difficult to hook, when hitting from downhill terrain and/or from a sidehill with the ball below your feet.

You will find it easier to hook, and more difficult to slice, if the terrain on which you stand is uphill and/or sidehill with the ball above your feet.

(I explain why these results tend to occur in Situation 8 where I talk about playing from uneven terrain.)

Situation 8

Situation: You face a shot from sloping terrain.

Suggestions: Almost any slope, no matter how slight, will affect the impact conditions. You will need to adjust your address position and/or your swing to take account of these special situations.

There are four basic types of sloping lies. There are the two sidehill situations, where your feet are more or less level with each other but higher or lower than the ball itself. And there are the uphill and downhill lies, where your left foot is either higher or lower than your right.

Uphill lie: Hitting up the slope creates the need for an upward angle of approach. This approach makes the ball fly higher and stop sooner than normal. The hillside inhibits leg action and therefore restricts the clearing of the left hip during the forward swing. Instead, the arms and hands tend to take over and close the clubface to the left prematurely. (*Adjustments:* Choose a club with less loft than normal. Aim it to the right of target. Set yourself perpendicular to the slope, with your right side lower and your left side higher than normal, as in *Illustration 35a*. Swing down the slope going back and up the slope going forward.)

Downhill lie: The downslope requires a steeply downward angle of approach. This makes the ball fly lower and run farther than normal. It also tends to leave the clubface open to the right at impact so that the ball slices in that direction. (*Adjustments:* Choose a more-lofted club. Aim for a left-to-right shot. Set up perpendicular to the slope—right side higher, left side lower than normal—as in *Illustration 35b*. Swing up the slope going back, down the slope going through.)

Sidehill lie (ball above feet): With the ball higher than the feet, you will need to address farther from the ball. This will create a flatter, more sweeping swing. The flatter swing tends to close the clubface to the left more abruptly than normal during the forward swing. (*Adjustments:* While standing on the slope, make several practice strokes until you find and can sense the flat, sweeping swing plane needed for solid contact. Then aim and align for a right-to-left ball flight and try to duplicate the flat swing that you sensed beforehand, as in *Illustration 35c*.)

Sidehill lie (ball below feet): A more upright swing than normal is needed for the clubhead to reach the bottom of the lower-sitting ball. The exaggerated upright swing, however, tends to make contact occur with the clubface open. (*Adjustments:* Stand closer to the ball and bend forward as needed for

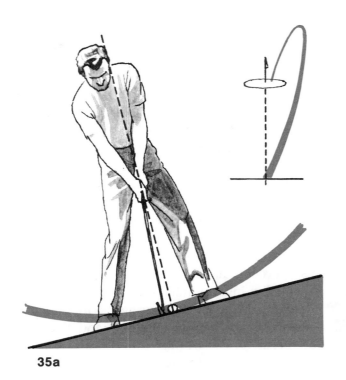

35a

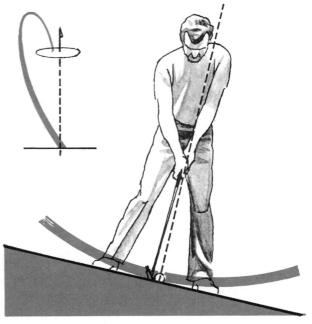

35b

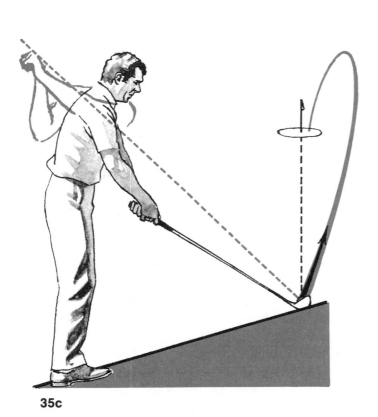

35c

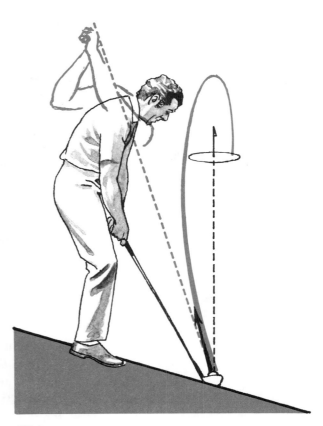

35d

the clubhead to reach ball level. Aim and align for the shot to fly from left to right, as in *Illustration 35d*. Swing the club largely with your arms and hands on a particularly upright, straight-line arc.)

FINAL
SUGGESTIONS:
EQUIPMENT,
PRACTICE,
ATTITUDE

In this final section I should like to discuss three subjects that I have not covered elsewhere in this book, namely equipment, practice and attitude. Hopefully I will bring forth some ways to help you improve your scoring with little or no conscious effort to actually change your golfing technique.

Equipment One simple and often successful way to immediately offset any tendency to slice or hook your shots would be to use clubs that have a different "lie" than you are now using.

The lie of a golf club is the angle formed between the underside of the shaft and a flat surface when the clubhead is soled on that surface. Any increase in that angle makes the club's lie more "upright." The shaft then extends more upward when the club is soled. Any decrease of that angle makes its lie that much "flatter." The shaft extends less upward.

The key relationships for you to remember are that a more upright lie in a given club tends to increase hooking or decrease slicing with that club (*Illustration 36b*). A flatter lie tends to decrease hooking or increase any slicing tendency (*Illustration 36a*).

Thus if slicing is your problem, you would want the lie of your wood clubs—especially your driver—and also your long and middle irons to be a little more upright than the manfacturer's standard. I would not suggest a more upright lie in the highly lofted irons, however, since the increased backspin applied with these clubs all but eliminates slicing anyway.

Conversely, if you tend to hook your shots, a flatter lie than standard would help to reduce or eliminate that problem.

Some club professionals have equipment on hand with which they can modify the lie of most iron clubs on the spot. Practically all manufacturers can supply customized sets of clubs in which all or certain ones of your choice feature lies that are more upright or flatter than standard.

I believe that most of today's driver clubs are too flat for the majority of golfers, most of whom tend to slice shots, especially with this particular club. I suspect that this trend toward flatter drivers has resulted to some extent from the influence of the touring professionals who are employed to represent and advise the manufacturers. Since hooking, not slicing, is the problem of most of these players, they naturally tend to favour the flatter lie.

Also, I have found that most club professionals tend to suggest more upright clubs for their taller golfers and flatter lies for their shorter players. While this makes sense in some cases, I feel that the individual's shot pattern is a more pertinent consid-

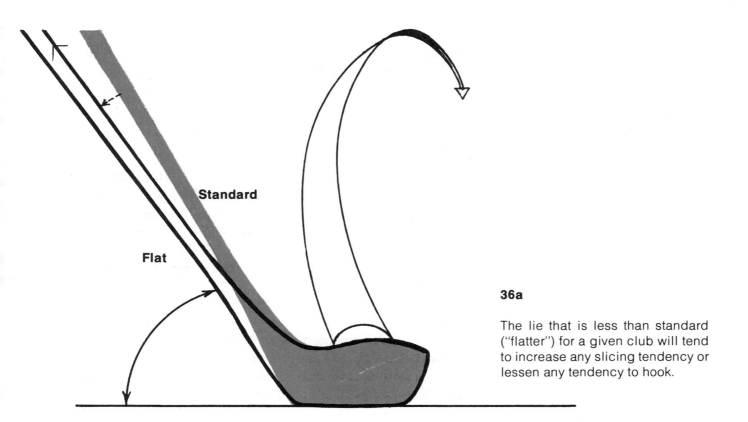

Standard

Flat

36a

The lie that is less than standard ("flatter") for a given club will tend to increase any slicing tendency or lessen any tendency to hook.

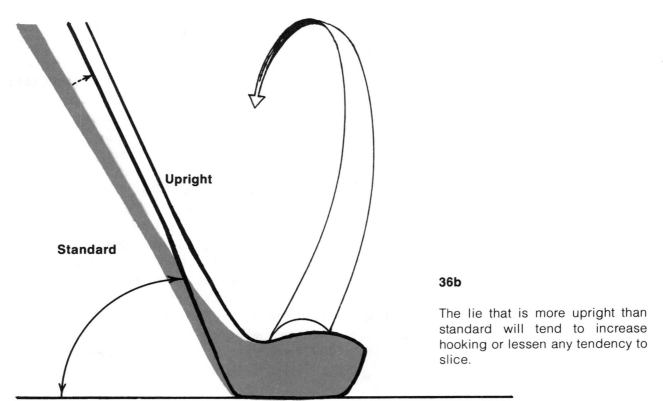

Upright

Standard

36b

The lie that is more upright than standard will tend to increase hooking or lessen any tendency to slice.

eration than his or her stature in deciding whether clubs should be upright or flat. I would never, for instance, suggest that a tall person use more upright clubs if he already hooks most of his shots. Nor would I advocate flatter clubs for a person who slices most shots, even though he be short in stature.

PRACTICE I would hope that many of my suggestions in this book will help you post lower scores, even if you should choose not to increase your practice time. Hopefully your shots will improve simply because you have a better picture of what your swing should be. You should also have a better understanding of what you can and should try—or cannot do and should not attempt—in certain situations.

Indeed, I have found that often I could improve my shots by merely thinking about and picturing my swing, perhaps while driving to a tournament, or while sitting in an armchair at home.

Also, I have found certain ways to make my actual practice time more productive. It is all too true in golf that lots of practice, if misspent, will not produce any improvement.

To make our practicing more productive, we could all benefit from the example set by Jack Nicklaus. I have never seen Jack hit a practice shot without first giving it the same careful thought that he would apply in a key competitive situation.

Without fail, he plans the shot and his execution of it before he ever steps up to the ball. He is particularly careful to aim the club and address the ball correctly, as you should be.

I suspect that this care taken in practice is a major reason why Jack competes so well under pressure. His routine on the course is the same as he has applied countless times in practice. The weekend golfer who does not practise as he plays feels lost to a certain degree on many shots that he must play on the course.

There is, however, one difference between the way you should practise and the way you should play. I suggest that you limit yourself in practice to no more than two thoughts during each swing. I suggest you limit yourself on the course to only one such thought. I would remind you to go through your address procedure on every shot prior to swinging.

I also believe that every golfer, even the nonpracticer, should hit at least a few shots before each round of play. This is vital, not only for getting the feel of a club in your hands, but also for finding your swing thought for the day. You will score better on average if you never walk onto the first tee without having first decided on the one thing you will think about as you swing the club.

Finally, a word about mastering a new swing technique through practice: do so initially with a club that you would not normally use for hitting shots a long distance. Choose a 6-iron or 7-iron rather than, say, a driver. Also, select a target that is about 20 yards closer than you would normally expect to hit shots with this club.

The reason for doing this is to make yourself swing at a tempo that is slow enough for your brain and body to perform an unfamiliar function. Adults, especially, need to swing at a brain speed that gives them time not only to do what the instructor has suggested, but also to sense—to feel—themselves doing it, so that they can repeat the correct feeling on future shots.

ATTITUDE

There is no doubt in my mind that lower scores will come about from improving both your impact conditions and your understanding of various on-course situations. I am equally certain, however, that almost all weekend golfers also need an improved attitude before they will ever play to their true potential.

Proper attitude in golf is probably a subject that is worthy of an entire book in itself. Here, however, as a final word in this text, I will mention three particular characteristics that dramatically separate, say, a Bobby Jones, a Ben Hogan, a Henry Cotton or a Bobby Locke from the average weekend player.

First, those great players were successful because they realized their limitations. They knew that some shots are all but impossible for anyone to play successfully. They knew that other shots were beyond their own particular abilities. Like great generals, they knew when to charge and when to retreat.

Though far less skilled, most weekend golfers that I have seen seldom retreat. I see them attempt shots that are doomed to fail in themselves, apart from the additional wasted strokes that they bring about. So learn to play within your limitations and attempt only those shots that you can reasonably expect to achieve, even if they might not be all that spectacular. Sometimes it's far better to accept the loss of one stroke instead of risking total disaster.

Second, you should work on developing the positive approach that is far more common among great players than among weekend golfers. Try to maintain the same attitude and degree of concentration that you adopt when you are two down with four holes to play. Avoid the negative thinking that comes when we are two up with four to go, or when we've just finished the front nine with a good score, the attitude that says, "I've got to be careful that I don't ruin everything with this one shot."

Finally, *try on every shot*. We are all determined to do our best on the first tee. We continue in this vein until disaster strikes, as it invariably does sooner or later. Then, so often, comes the blowup.

Continuing with your best effort after running into trouble—and succeeding as a result—is surely the best way to get the maximum satisfaction from playing golf. Come to think of it, the same would hold true of life itself.

About the Authors

John Jacobs played golf professionally in the 1950s and was captain of the British Ryder Cup team. Since then he has established an international reputation as a master analyst and teacher, instructing top pros and weekend golfers around the world. Jacobs is the author of numerous books including the classic *Practical Golf.*

Dick Aultman was a longtime contributing editor to *Golf Digest.* He collaborated with Bob Toski, Gary Player, Lee Trevino, and Sam Snead, among many others, to write more than a dozen golf books.